The Gift of Divine Guidance

The Gift of Divine Guidance

From the Soul of an Artist

Lucille Edgarian

BALBOA.
PRESS
A DIVISION OF HAY HOUSE

Balboa Press books may be ordered through booksellers or by contacting:

Balboa Press
A Division of Hay House
1663 Liberty Drive
Bloomington, IN 47403
www.balboapress.com
1-(877) 407-4847

ISBN: 978-1-4525-4817-3 (sc)
ISBN: 978-1-4525-4819-7 (hc)
ISBN: 978-1-4525-4818-0 (e)

Printed in the United States of America

Balboa Press rev. date:3/9/2012

For my spirit guardian, who has guided me since childhood and even now helped in getting this book published

Contents

PREFACE

This is a true story. Although it is spiritual and inspirational, it is also historical. It covers many unforgettable events that took place between 1928 and 1995. The women's issues that abound in the story are not for the faint of heart because they will evoke strong emotions. The supernatural episodes that take place are all factual. They reveal the mystical side of life that we still do not fully comprehend.

The story begins in 1928, during The Great Depression, with my unusual birth. The difficult times during my early years were filled with incessant hardships. Out of necessity, when I was four years old, Mother had to take my sister Theresa and me to a convent to live, where we remained for the next eight grueling years. The humiliation, strict punishments, and abuse that I was subjected to nearly shattered my human spirit.

Fortunately, when I was five years old, I discovered an unusual form of meditation that resulted in a spiritual experience and opened my awareness to a divine source of help. A spiritual presence became my guardian. This comforting guidance enabled me to endure the difficult periods that I was often subjected to, and it helped in giving me the sheer determination to develop an unconquerable character.

At a young age, I discovered a natural ability to draw, which became the foundation for a deep desire to become an artist. That interest was an escape at first, until it developed into an obsession in wanting to learn everything I possibly could about painting. The passion I felt in wanting to accomplish my goal was aided by unexpected opportunities. They eventually lead me into developing unusual works that can only be described as inspired by a divine source. The artistic pursuits I sought are not only informative but educational as well.

As an adult, I encountered countless hardships, and gut wrenching heartbreaks. I was able to survive the stressful and often painful ordeals I had to overcome only by seeking the aid of my spiritual guardian, whom I consciously began to rely on more and more. Through meditation, I learned to fine-tune my intuition, the source that guided me into making the right decisions.

The story is written from the soul of an artist and is intended to inspire those who believe in the spirit. It is a mere example of what can be accomplished when we are open to the divine source that is available to all of us.

ACKNOWLEDGMENTS

I first want to thank my three wonderful children, Linda, Debbie, and Arty, for enriching my life. Their constant love, devotion, and support brought me countless blessings that saw me through unimaginable difficult periods.

My heartfelt gratitude goes to my daughter Debbie, who encouraged me to learn to use the computer. As the principal of an elementary school, she still found time to make herself available to help me in countless ways—from formatting and editing to typing. Mainly, she taught me everything I learned about the use of a computer during the ten years that it took to complete my story.

A special thank you is especially given to my daughter Linda, whose support, expert advice, editing, and constant revisions helped bring this work to its conclusion. In spite of her busy schedule as a full-time middle-school teacher, she always took time to answer my calls and give me her invaluable assistance.

To my dear friend, Nelda Montgomery, a huge thanks for her encouragement and support. Her tireless typing of the early drafts and writing query letters, and her research for locating literary agents was invaluable. I am sorry to say, she passed away before my work was finished.

I want to acknowledge and thank my niece Kristen McLane, who devoted many hours to assisting me the first year I began writing. Her excitement in wanting to have this story told made me persevere in spite of all the setbacks.

My editor, Lana Castle, deserves special recognition for her invaluable assistance and her tireless input during the final stages of helping me rewrite my manuscript.

I am forever indebted to my husband Bill for his never-waning patience and encouragement, and especially for the many times he had to prepare lunches and dinners to keep us from going hungry in order to keep me focused.

1

LUCILLE

On a sultry June afternoon in Manchester, New Hampshire, the woman's screams could be heard throughout the apartment building. Lillian had been in labor for nearly twenty hours and was in a state of anguish. Finally, the baby seemed ready to make its entrance, and the doctor was summoned.

Anxiously waiting for the doctor to arrive, the midwife boiled water while Lillian's mother paced the floor, praying the doctor would arrive soon to put her daughter out of her misery. Lillian's husband, Dominic Therrien, wondered why this delivery was so difficult, since the birth of his daughter Theresa sixteen months before had gone so smoothly.

The doctor arrived at last, and after examining Lillian, his face reflected his fear. This was a breech baby. Knowing that time was of the essence, he reached inside the birth canal and succeeded in pulling her out. Lillian's agony stopped when the baby girl was released from her cocoon, still encased in the placenta. As an old wives-tale proclaims, she was born with a "veil," a sign that she would be endowed with psychic abilities and many talents.

This baby was me, getting ready to come into this world. I must have known the misery I would encounter in life and decided to delay my first earthly breath. No one in their right mind would have chosen to be born during the Great Depression that was taking place in 1928, but that was my fate.

I was told years later that I was a bundle of screaming energy with hair as black as a raven and eyes the color of dark chocolate. Long before my birth, my parents decided to name me Lucille. By adding their last name, Therrien, my name could loosely be interpreted as meaning "Heavenly and Earthly."

Within minutes of my delivery, there was a knock at the apartment door, followed by a constant pounding. Several men began shouting in unison, "Open up, it's the police!"

My father suspected why they were there, quickly ran to gather his homemade booze, and hid it under the birthing bed before opening the door. An established custom of the times was that men were not allowed to enter the bedroom of a woman in labor—especially just after she gave birth. When the police peeked in and saw Mother with a new baby suckling at her breast, they quickly excused themselves. The officers meticulously searched the rest of the rooms, and finding nothing to confiscate, left the apartment building.

My father felt pretty smug because they had not found the illegal booze, especially since it was not the first time the police had raided the house. He suspected a nosy neighbor must have reported him for the reward offered for that offence. Jobs in this town known for its textile mills and shoe factories were nonexistent, and the newly formed prohibition created a demand for booze. Many men made liquor to sell in their bathtub. Often it was their only means of making some money to feed their families.

Those were difficult times, and my desperate father was known to solve his problems the easy yet often illegal way.

After the police left, my father waited an hour. When all was clear, he walked into Mother's bedchamber and gathered the afterbirth. He tiptoed down the two flights of stairs and walked behind the building. He glanced around to be certain he had not been seen, then carefully buried the afterbirth and made the sign of the cross for protection.

Five months after my birth, Mother discovered she was pregnant again. When she was in her third month of pregnancy, she and my father left a happy family gathering and were walking home in the middle of a snowstorm. My father had been drinking heavily, as usual, and when they were within a mile of their house, he started an argument that escalated into a terrible fight. Unable to control his rage, he began slapping my mother repeatedly. She cowered, tried to resist him, and pleaded with him to stop, but that enraged him even more. He repeatedly punched her until she fell into the snow. Now consumed with an uncontrollable anger, he kicked her until she was a bloody mess. The last punch across her face was so hard that it knocked out her front teeth. Seeing the red pool forming on the white snow jarred his senses and made him aware of what he had done. Frightened and in a state of panic, he began to run, believing he had killed her. Mother was left in the snow unconscious with blood pooling around her.

A short time later, a young couple walking through the field spotted a dark object ahead of them. They approached cautiously and were shocked to find a badly beaten woman. They began rubbing her hands and talked to her until she opened her eyes. Looking around and still in a daze, Mother told the young couple what had happened. They carefully lifted her and helped her walk to her mother's house a few blocks away.

Upon seeing her daughter's battered face, my grandmother began crying and put her to bed. She sent her son for the doctor and thanked the couple for rescuing her. Within ten minutes, the doctor arrived. His first concern was making sure that the baby Mother was carrying was all right. He bandaged her many wounds and gave her some pain medicine. He then came to check on me and my older sister Theresa. Before going home, the doctor reported the incident to the police, who issued a warrant for my father's arrest.

When Mother was well enough, Grandmother laid down the law to her, saying, "Enough! I'm not going to continue to watch you get treated this way! You must decide to either leave him or stay with him when he is found. The choice is yours, but if you choose to stay with him, don't come back here crying, telling me about your miserable life."

Mother chose to leave him. That's when we moved in with Grandmother, Grandfather, Uncle Oliver, and Aunt Lucy.

A month passed by before the police located my father. They had to let him go because Mother was so afraid of him she would not press charges. Before he was released, the police gave him a strict warning.

"Get out of town, and don't ever try to come back here. If you do, you will be arrested and thrown in jail."

That ended any further contact Mother had with him. The family was relieved to be rid of him, especially my mother, who now felt safe.

Fourteen months after my birth, Mother gave birth to the baby she had been carrying when my father had beat her. Thankfully, he was a healthy, beautiful boy. She named him Emile. We were now three babies and five adults all living in a cramped apartment.

During this time, my grandfather was gravely ill and unable to work, placing the burden of providing for the family on my grandmother. She had to work twelve to fourteen hours a day in a shoe factory under deplorable conditions to receive a meager salary at the end of the week. It was barely enough to pay the bills. Now with the addition of three children under the age of five and my mother, who was not able to work, the financial hardships my family had to endure compounded.

A few months later, my beloved grandfather passed away. I spent several days wondering why he would not wake up from inside the beautiful box displayed in our living room. I tried to talk to him many times, but the grownups who came to see him would shush me, saying I must be quiet because Grandpa had gone to heaven. I had no idea what they were talking about. His passing was hard on the family, but it ended up being a blessing because the many medical expenses his illness had required were eliminated, giving Grandmother some extra money she desperately needed.

One evening in 1929, Grandmother and Mother were listening to the radio when they both burst into tears. I was too young to understand that a devastating crisis had just occurred. The stock market had crashed. This financial calamity affected the thousands of people in our city and across the United States. Many were left destitute when factories had to close. Banks closed too, when investors took their money out and left other investors without their savings. It was chaos on a national scale. By December 1930, just a few weeks before Christmas, the United States Bank went bankrupt.

Mother's financial situation reached a critical state. She could not find a job, and with three children to take care of daily, it was impossible. Even worse, the Parish priest informed her that the church could no longer provide her with extra food. He explained that too many people were in the same situation. It was a hopeless predicament; everywhere she went to seek some help she was turned away.

Eventually, the government in Washington, D.C., funded a new relief program. In our city, the mayor was in charge of allocating the meager funds to families he believed were in desperate need and required immediate assistance.

Mother kept trying and once again went to see the mayor to plead for help. She prayed that this time she would qualify for the new relief program. His first response was to inform her he had spoken with the parish priest, and even though she had three children, they could not help her.

After a few weeks, the mayor, knowing the gravity of Mother's situation, met with the parish priest again with an idea. If the priest found a suitable place that would accept my sister Theresa and me and would agree not to separate us, the state would pay for our upkeep. The priest promised he would keep us together and arranged for Theresa and me to be taken to a local French convent. The next day the mayor signed the necessary papers and made us wards of the state. Our brother Emile, then three years old, was too young to be accepted in the convent, so he was boarded out to various relatives.

2

MY SPIRITUAL GUARDIAN

Even though I was only four years old at the time, I recall the event as if it happened yesterday. I can still see myself sitting on the kitchen table while Mother fastens the buttons on my black patent leather shoes. Tears are falling from her eyes and splashing onto my shoes. The wonderful smell of Grandmother's freshly baked apple pie permeates the air. As I look across the room, I see Grandmother in her rocking chair with Theresa on her lap. She is singing a French song I recognize as one she usually sings when she is sad. While I listen to her, I can tell something is wrong because my tummy begins to feel funny. As I experience my first pangs of fear, I immediately begin to cry. *"Mama, pour quoi tu pleur?"* "Mother, why are you crying?"

I ask in a trembling voice, but she cannot answer me through her sobs. Watching the tears flow down her cheeks, I can no longer control my own tears and begin wailing. Before long, we are all sobbing uncontrollably. A sense of foreboding tells me something really bad is about to happen.

Later in the day, I remember Mother carrying a suitcase and holding on to Theresa's left hand, while I'm holding Theresa's right hand. It seems like we walked a very long time before we arrived at a huge house. The size of it frightened me so much that I almost wet my pants. As we climbed the stairs, Theresa and I clung to Mother's skirt. Instinctively, I knew this had to be the reason why Mother had been crying while she was getting me dressed. Mother located a key-like knob that protruded from the door, and when she twisted it, it sounded like a bell. I held my breath and squeezed my eyes shut, not wanting to see what was going to happen next. Within a few seconds, a person in a long black robe opened the door. Theresa and I began to scream and cry at the same time. Mother tried to calm us by saying, "Don't cry, girls. This is a very nice nun, and she is going to take good care of you. She will be like a new grandmother!"

All I could see was a big, tall person covered in black. I did not know what a nun was and wailed all the louder when she came close to me. I gripped Mother's skirt even tighter while she tried to pry my hands away. With a sweet smile on her face, the nun called one of the older girls to come and calm us. The girl appeared to be about thirteen years old and was quite pretty. She had unusual blue eyes, and her hair was the color of matured wheat. Her beautiful smile put us at ease momentarily. She said her name was Agnes. Her friendliness lowered our guard, and she succeeded in prying our hands away from Mother's skirt. In a soft voice, she invited us to follow her to the kitchen for some cookies and milk. For an added enticement, Agnes held up a bunch of red grapes for us to eat along the way. Since this was the first time we had seen or eaten grapes, we were captivated by their delicious taste. Mother took advantage of our being distracted and urged us to go with Agnes to see what else she had to give us.

"I will wait for you right here," she told us.

Theresa and I felt uneasy but followed Agnes to the kitchen, looking back every now and then to make sure Mother was still there. Once we were out of sight, she seized the opportunity to leave.

When we discovered that Mother was gone, Theresa and I imagined we would never see her again. My chest felt strange, and I wondered if my heart was breaking inside. We were two lost lambs frightened beyond belief and inconsolable for days. Two weeks went by before we saw her again because the nun had convinced Mother it was the best thing to do, telling her it would help us adjust to our new surroundings if she stayed away for a while.

It took many weeks for me to adjust because the change from a happy, loving home to the strict, regimented life I was thrust into was mystifying and confusing. For the first time in my life, I felt the pangs of being abandoned. Somewhat like a bird falling out of a tree before it is ready to fly, I experienced the frightening helplessness only a child can know.

Within a few days, I learned that the big house where Mother had taken us was a French-speaking convent. At the age of four, I was the youngest child they had allowed to live there. One reason was because I did not wet the bed at night. The minimum age up to this time had been five. The other reason was because the nuns made an exception in my case. They promised the priest and the mayor that they would not separate Theresa and me.

After we had been in the convent a month, I found out that Mother came every Saturday with a suitcase filled with a change of clothes for us to wear the following week. The nuns would cleverly keep us busy in another part of the building so we would not see her when she came. The many years we lived in the convent, we never once saw our mother on Saturday.

Visiting hours were strictly observed—after lunch on Sunday from one o'clock until four. We did get to leave the premises for that short period, but no excuses were allowed for returning late. If you were late even by a few minutes, the punishment was the same: you were not permitted to see your parent the following Sunday. There was a punishment for everything without consideration for uncontrollable circumstances. During Mother's visits, our time was limited, so we chose activities close by. My favorite place was the drugstore around the corner from the convent because it offered ice cream cones and root beer floats.

Some Sundays we ventured a little further and visited the five-and-ten-cent store nearby, mainly to gaze at the toys. Once in a great while if Mother was able to save a few extra pennies, she bought us some big white peppermints. At a nickel per pound, she could afford half a pound and had the storekeeper divide them into two separate bags, one for Theresa, and the other for me. I grew up loving their taste, but more importantly, the smell of peppermint to this day reminds me of Mother because she always had some in her purse.

Theresa and I learned to hide our mints, usually in the top part of our stockings but sometimes in our underpants, because the first time we went back to the convent with them, the nun searched us and took them away. We were told that no one should have more than another. If the other girls did not have what we had, then we could not have them either. This was their way of doing away with jealousy or envy. I suspected that when they took away our mints, or anything else for that matter, they must have kept them for themselves.

To give you a glimpse of what life was like for us back then, our typical days would start by getting up at five a.m. We had to learn to wash ourselves with our nightgown on, then dress or undress under our nightgowns as well. Believe me, this took a lot of practice. After getting dressed, we had to make our beds.

The beds were smaller than twin-size, and each had a matching white damask spread and a white linen pillow sham. The sheets had to be pulled firmly on the sides, so tight that a tossed comb would bounce on it. If it did not bounce, we had to make the bed over again. The older girls were in charge of inspecting this morning ritual. Once in a while, the nun in charge inspected. If the bed was not made to her liking, she would pull the bedding apart and have us redo it. This took time, and we would end up missing breakfast. By the time I was seven, I had missed quite a few morning meals and became thin and frail looking.

All the chores took place after breakfast. Every day we were given a different assignment: clean up the dining room, wash the dishes, dust, or mop the floors. Others were told to clean the blackboard erasers. This was considered a treat because we were allowed to go outside. My favorite job was dusting the stairs because I could sit while I was working and take my sweet time to dust all around the wooden spokes.

Once a month the nuns would wash the hardwood floors and apply paste wax. The girls who were selected to buff the floors were lucky because it became a playful escape. I was picked a few times when I was older. The thrill of putting on thick, white, wool socks and being allowed to run across the room and slide on the wood to make the floor shine like a mirror was exhilarating. Even though this was supposed to be work, we shrieked with laughter as we deliberately fell on our behinds, and the freedom of the moment was refreshing, breaking the heavy, austere environment we had become accustomed to.

When I entered the convent, I was too young to be in a structured classroom, so I was assigned to one of the older nuns, who watched over me during the class periods. Her name was Sister Carmel. She was a bit plump, with rosy cheeks and a perpetual smile. Her booming laugh made me tingle with happiness. She was known to be the kindest nun in the convent, and before too long she became like a grandmother to me.

In the early years, Sister Carmel would take me to her room on the third floor every day. She would read to me, and when I got sleepy, she would rock me until I fell asleep. I learned that she had a spark of mischief in her and enjoyed defying some of the rules. For example, one day she gave me a piece of Beech-Nut chewing gum—a definite no-no. Putting her finger to her mouth, she said, "Shhh, don't tell anybody! This will be our big secret."

It was the first time I was told to keep a secret, and it felt special. After tasting the gum, believe me, I was not about to tell a soul, not wanting to miss out on the next time I might be given another piece of that delicious gum.

When I was a little older, Sister Carmel began giving me pieces of fabric that I could use to make doll clothes. I hid them in the top of my stockings and snuck them in the assembly room where we had sewing sessions. Sadly, one day the supervising nun caught me stuffing fabric scraps Sister Carmel had given me into my assigned sewing bag. Being suspicious, she accused me of stealing the fabric from the nuns' quarters. She demanded that I tell her who I had taken them from. I did not want Sister Carmel to get into trouble, knowing that she was not supposed to give me things, so I just stood there and wouldn't answer her. My defiance infuriated her even more. When she saw that I was not going to tell her, she dragged me by the arm down the stairs until we reached the basement. She opened the locked furnace room and forcibly threw me in it, then quickly locked the door. While still in the hallway she screamed, "You will stay in there until you tell me who you stole the fabric from!"

This being my first time in the furnace room, I was traumatized. I could hear the loud furnace turning on and shutting off. Not knowing what the exploding noise was in the pitch-blackness, I crouched closer to the door and brought my knees up to my chest to have something to hold on to. I pounded on the door and started shouting, "Let me out! Let me out!"

But the nun had already gone back upstairs, and no one was around to hear me.

When a rat ran across my legs I swatted him away. Feeling his coarse hair on my fingers made my own hair tingle as if bugs were crawling on my scalp. I could hear the rats screeching, and when another one crawled up my arm toward my face, I flung him away. That's when I began shaking. The glow coming from the furnace door was creating dark shadows and forming strange patterns on the walls, making me think the devil was in the room. I moaned and cried for hours to no avail.

Sister Carmel eventually heard from one of the other nuns that the commotion taking place in the basement involved me, her charge. Being one of the older nuns with authority, she had me removed from my dungeon and demanded that one of the older girls bring me to her room. I spent the night enveloped in her big arms. She tried to console me, but I could not get the evil pictures in my mind to go away and could not stop shaking or calm down. That hellish day stayed with me for a very long time.

There were many other episodes of being thrown in the furnace room, since this was one of the nuns' favorite punishments. I suppose it was their way of trying to control us, thinking that by creating such fear, we would submit to any demand.

As the second and third years progressed, I was well indoctrinated into the routines and schedules of my new life. The younger girls, ages five through nine, were sent to bed earlier than the older girls, usually by six-thirty p.m. By the time the twenty or so girls used the only toilet in the dormitory, washed up, and got into bed, it would have taken over an hour. When the next group of girls, from age ten through twelve, arrived to perform the same ritual, followed by the many teenagers, it would be very late.

My bed happened to be the third one from the sinks. With all the noise going on around me, I was unable to fall asleep. After lying in bed a while, I developed the habit of staring at the bare light bulb that hung from the ceiling above the sinks. I would do this every night. Over time, when I stared at the light bulb, I began to see events take place in my mind, and I noticed that by staring at the light a long time, I would easily go into a trance-like state. The more I stared at the light, the faster things began flashing through my mind. I saw places I had been and distinctly remembered having lived on earth before. Another night, I experienced being able to fly, and I saw myself flying to different places and going through doors without opening them. After that experience, I started jumping down from the top of the stairs trying to make myself fly, but I always ended up hurting myself, so I reluctantly gave up that practice.

After lying in bed awhile, I learned to project my thoughts to another place, and instantly, I would be there. I could look down and see people, but they could not see me. It was a marvelous discovery to be able to float near the ceiling. I could lower myself or rise higher by just thinking about it. I also seemed to remember knowledge that I had learned in a previous lifetime.

I was surprised one night when I was in a trance state to hear a distinct voice telling me not to be afraid. I was told I was being watched over and would be protected. After that night, being sent to bed early became a blessing and a means of escape from my tormentors. I now looked forward to being able to communicate with my newly discovered spiritual guardian. It was like living in two worlds. I learned that if I focused on the light bulb until my eyes became blurry, a misty white light would envelope me and take me into a meditative state. At that moment, I was no longer in the bedroom but in another dimension. I began purposely going into this other dimension every night, and while there, I was made aware of this spiritual guardian that confirmed he would comfort and guide me when needed. Before long, I found I could capture the same experience by just staring fixedly out a window or at a spot across the room. I began seeing things that would happen days or even months later. One day, since I was a child and still very trusting, I told a nun something bad was going to happen. I told her that one of the nuns was going to die. With a sneer on her face she replied, "Lucille, where do you get those foolish ideas from?"

I wasn't about to tell her, so I just shrugged my shoulders and lowered my head. She accepted it as a child's fantasy and gave me a stern look. When a nun died unexpectedly of a cerebral hemorrhage a few weeks later, the nun I had spoken to began questioning me more seriously. I told her the truth by saying it had come into my head by itself. I did not want her to know how I knew. After that episode, she was convinced I was possessed by the devil and treated me accordingly.

On another occasion, one of the girls lost a mitten. Everybody was asked to look for it. While everyone was looking, I just stared into space. In my mind, I saw the mitten in a boot way in the back of the clothes closet. I told the nun where to find the lost mitten, and sure enough, there it was. Well, that revelation got me into some serious trouble. She asked me how I knew the mitten was there. I told her I had seen it in my head. She did not believe me of course and said I must have put it there myself. She now accused me not only of being a liar but a thief as well. My punishment for lying was to be sent to the dreaded furnace room for the rest of the day. From that day on, I decided it was better for me to keep my thoughts to myself.

This time, while in the dark dreaded room listening to the roar of the furnace, I began to tremble with fear. Then a serene calm came over me, and the room was engulfed in a warm golden glow. I instinctively sensed it was my spiritual guardian who watched over me with his comforting presence. I was not afraid of being in the furnace room anymore, even while listening to the rats and the weird noises. A short time later, I actually fell asleep. Whenever I was thrown into the dark furnace room after that, which happened quite often, I did not scream anymore because my thoughts propelled me to another place, and I would feel my guardian close by assuring me of his protected trust.

The nun could not understand the change in me, and again branded me the child of the devil. She told all the girls that night to pray for me because the devil had entered my body and soul. One nun even wrote my name on a piece of paper and placed it under the statue of the Blessed Virgin for protection. My sister Theresa's name was also under the statue quite often. I'm sure we were both singled out for unwarranted punishments, and I could not understand why we were treated differently. I guess it was because we were wards of the state. The girls whose parents were doctors or business owners were treated differently. Some of the older girls who were residents in training to become nuns were given special favors all the time. Many of them looked down on Theresa and me as if we were low class and not good enough to socialize with them.

This same disdain and humiliating treatment was extended to the other girls who were also wards of the state. Those were the girls I chose as my friends. Yet, even with them, I had to be on my guard because they could easily be enticed to switch alliances by one of the special girls or by a nun in exchange for a reward or special favor. Thank goodness, Theresa and I had each other. It made life in the convent more tolerable.

3

FAMILY

On November 8, 1932, Franklin Delano Roosevelt was elected President of the United States. He ran on the promise that he would help improve the lives of the American people and the country as a whole. He called his program of reform The New Deal that would become a hands-on government program. Congress established the Civilian Conservation Corps. The CCC created many new jobs. My Uncle Oliver seized the opportunity to work for the organization and was trained as a field cook.

Another benefit the Civilian Conservation Corps inadvertently provided was, it opened up jobs for women. Mother at last was hired at one of the textile mills in town that was subsidized by government contracts. The pay was meager: not even a dollar a week, but it helped a great deal. Being young and healthy, Mother also cleaned houses at night for some of the wealthy families. Her workdays lasted fourteen to sixteen hours, six days a week in order to make ends meet. Mother believed my sister and I were being well cared for in the convent, and that made it possible for her to work those long hours.

Eleanor Roosevelt began speaking out for women's rights. As the wife of our new president, she carried a lot of weight and encouraged women to get involved to improve their lives. Women's sufferance began in earnest, and the right to vote was finally voted through. Unions were formed to protect the working class against the unfair practices of factory owners. As a group, women became a force to be reckoned with, demanding equal rights for all citizens not just for men. Mother was involved and marched in some of the parades for these great causes.

As the years went by, her English-speaking skills improved, and gradually she learned to read and write in English, an accomplishment she was proud of. Even though Mother still lived with my grandmother, her life began to improve.

The convent closed during the Christmas holidays. Even though we never had a decorated Christmas tree and no presents, the thrill of being reunited with the people we loved was better than any gift. Strange as it may seem, we did not miss what we never had, nor did we think we were being deprived.

The only other time we left the convent was during the summer, when the convent closed for the months of July and August. During the first few years, Theresa and I stayed with different aunts or cousins who were in a position to take care of us. Sadly, those were not happy times. It was obvious that some did not care for us out of love but rather for the money Mother paid them. Several aunts were as strict as the nuns and just as mean.

As Theresa and I grew older, we had to constantly be on guard because some of the uncles would try to molest us. Their sweet, low voices were always a telltale sign of what they had on their minds. They would ask us to fondle them, or say, "Come here and give your uncle a kiss."

They were sneaky and thought we were gullible. Some would even offer us money so we would not tell what they tried to do. Luckily, Theresa and I had been brought up to tell the truth, and we confided in each other. This gave us the needed strength to form an alliance against those predators. With our strict upbringing, we knew what those uncles tried to do was wrong, so we'd report their behavior to the aunt in charge of us at the time. This always caused a family problem, and we would end up being taken to another relative. Many times, the aunt just didn't want to be bothered with children.

As Theresa and I grew older, we required less attention. This made it possible for us to start spending the summer months with Aunt Delia. She and her husband Medy lived on a big farm about thirty-five miles outside of town. Uncle Medy was a hard worker. He had started with very little, but with hard work and a fierce driving force, he purchased their hundred plus acres. With the help of some friends, he built a three-story house that became one of the most beautiful Victorian-style houses in the area.

Those two months in the summer were not only enjoyable but were the greatest education a child could have. I learned to appreciate nature, its beauty, and the many lessons only nature can provide. Seeing and experiencing close up the many kinds of animals and smelling the scents of barn life, freshly cut hay, and countless other things still remain in my senses. Even today, those familiar smells bring back fond memories. As one summer followed another, the wonder of it all made a big impact on me.

One curious but fond memory I have of Aunt Delia is that she kept a chamber pot in her bedroom. This was before indoor plumbing. Every morning she took it outside and watered her roses with the previous night's contents. She ended up having the biggest and most beautiful roses you ever saw, and those roses were her pride and joy.

Another bonus we enjoyed while living on the farm was that it gave Mother a chance to visit us more often. Working as much as she did, whenever she had a free day, she would come out and spend the time with us. Because the farm was far from town, she had to find someone who had a car to drive her out there. Her visits were wonderful because she could stay as long as she wanted, not the three meager hours we were allowed on Sunday in the convent, with strict dictates to be back at a certain time. This gave Theresa and me the opportunity to get to know our mother personally in a more relaxed home environment for the first time in our young lives. We looked forward to having her close, hoping it would sooth our longing for her, but somehow, she felt more like a friend than a mother.

4

CONVENT LIFE

Whenever summer ended, I dreaded returning to the convent, with its austere confines and its never-ending strict rules. As I aged, I was able to control the beatings somewhat, but the frustration and anger some of the nuns exhibited was often instantaneous and unpredictable.

One particular incident stands out in my mind. A boy in my third grade class was not feeling well. He put his head down on the desk to find relief from the fever that was burning his face. The nun walked by and, thinking he was taking a nap, told him to sit up straight. He was so sick that he just stayed in that position. Without warning, the nun spun around, grabbed him by the hair on the top of his head, lifted him up, and flung him across the room. A hunk of the boy's hair remained in her hand. The entire class sat there unable to move, in a state of shock, afraid to make a sound. I began shaking, knowing she was out of control, and wondering who would be next.

That same boy was sick quite often and usually carried a tin of salve for sores. Many times, I saw him eat the salve. It was common knowledge that he ran away from the convent periodically, but since his mother was unable to take care of him, she would always bring him back. A few months after the hair-pulling episode, I noticed that he did not come to class one day. While the nun was busy, one of the boys was able to pass a note around the room, and that's how we learned that poor little boy had hung himself. He was only eight years old. The night before, he had climbed up a rope that hung down from one of the swings in the boys' yard, and taking the other rope, he wound it around his neck and let go. The next morning they found his lifeless body.

I think it was during this period that I began pulling my hair out because I had become a nervous wreck. I would pull one hair at a time in the area called the widow's peak. I kept doing this so much and for such a long time that it eventually formed into a scab the size of a quarter. When my grandmother heard about it, she pleaded with me to stop. As an incentive, she promised to give me a fountain pen when she knew I did not do it anymore.

We had courses in penmanship at the time, and I had to share a pen with the girl who sat next to me. That always annoyed me because I had to wait a long time for my turn. The lure of owning my own fountain pen was the best incentive Grandmother could have given me, but pulling my hair out had become such a bad habit, it took me three months to finally stop. Unfortunately, the damage I caused was permanent, and my widow's peak never grew back.

Sister Alma, who was usually in charge of the girls, was known to be especially cruel and impatient. One morning I approached her desk and asked a question. Without looking up, she told me to go back to my seat. I hesitated to go back because she had not answered me. Apparently, I did not move fast enough because the next thing I knew, she had me by the back of the neck. Squeezing her long fingernails deep into the flesh of my neck, she flung me across the room. The burning pain I felt was so intense, I began screaming. The next day I saw her nails had left five long tracks on the sides of my neck that later formed scabs and took months to heal.

Another favorite punishment of Sister Alma's was to have us extend our hands palms down. She would strike our knuckles hard with the metal edge of a ruler, repeating the strikes with more force each time. It hurt so much that our tears flowed in spite of trying to show no emotion and remembering we had to endure her strikes in silence in order to avoid worse punishments. The bloody welts the metal edge left took weeks to heal, and the swelling lasted for days.

One afternoon, when I was around eight years old, I was on my way to the dormitory to put something away when this same nun stopped me. I must have answered her in a way she didn't like because the next thing

I knew, she had the long-handled radiator brush in her hand, pinning me down on the stairs. She began striking me with the handle of the brush in a crazed fury, hitting me across my back, the top of my head, and the back of my neck. After a few minutes of this repeated barrage, I turned around and said, "Jesus would be very angry with you if he knew how mean you are to me and to the other children."

This enraged her even more, and she continued hitting me. She hit me wherever she could strike. I finally escaped her cruelty for a moment and ran up the stairs, trying to get away from her, but she was faster than I was and lunged to catch me midway up the stairs. By now, her anger was beyond control. The blows found my shoulders and arms. Her careless strikes stung my legs and neck. I tried to protect my head with my hands, for she seemed to be more intent on hitting it, but my hands were not fast enough to stop the painful blows. Instinctively, I stopped trying to protect myself, and a calm feeling came over me. I just lay there limp while she kept striking me with all her strength. Turning my head, I stared intently into her eyes with a piercing glare. This made her arm freeze in midair as she was about to strike again. Now at last, with a surprised look on her face, she became aware of what she was doing and lowered her arm. With a shaking voice filled with hatred she screamed, "Go to bed this instant."

I must have passed out because I don't remember going up the stairs. I will never forget the feeling I experienced the moment I stopped trying to protect myself—it was the same as when I was in the furnace room a few years before. The same golden light surrounded me, and a calm voice told me to stop fighting and let go, assuring me that I would be all right. This convinced me at last that my unseen guardian was constantly watching over me and had come to protect me once again.

Life at times seemed unbearable, yet I managed to survive mainly because of my belief in my spiritual guardian. Theresa and I tried many times to tell our mother about the beatings and the other severe punishments when she came on Sundays, but it was fruitless. The nun in charge always denied it and fabricated a story that convinced our mother we were lying. Invariably, after Mother left, we were punished even more for telling. After a while, we learned to keep our mouths shut to protect ourselves.

I must say, there were some fun times too. For example, when I was six years old, I discovered the desire to draw. I began drawing whenever I had a chance and would sketch for hours. That's when I started developing my natural talent. I found that, whenever I sketched, I would go into a serene place within myself. I now preferred to stay by myself and draw to capture that wonderful feeling of freedom. I taught myself to copy all the pictures I saw from the books I read and became very good at copying just about anything.

When I was in the third grade, I won a drawing contest. I spent hours drawing an Indian in full headdress from a picture in our history book. The picture was two inches square, and my drawing was eleven by fourteen inches. It was done in pencil, and my shading gave it great dimension. When the nun looked at it, she immediately wanted to disqualify me, accusing me of having traced it. I had to prove to her that I had not traced it by showing her the photo in the history book. This convinced her there was no way I could have traced it, since my drawing was much larger. Subsequently, I received the First Place Award. What a thrill it was to have entered and won my first art competition!

After that, drawing became my obsession. It was a way for me to go within and capture the same feeling I experienced when I stared at a light source. That habit intensified through the years, and I was now aware that if I simply stared at a given spot, not just at the bedroom light bulb, I could project myself into another dimension at will. This phenomenon happened naturally whenever I got lost in thought, especially when I was engrossed in sketching.

About this same period, my eyesight began to get hazy. Theresa and I sang in the children's choir every Sunday, and we had weekly rehearsals. During rehearsals one day, I was unable to see the words. When the nun called on me to sing a duet, I couldn't. She thought I was kidding. After I convinced her I was not joking, she excused me from the choir. Later that week, Mother took me to an eye doctor, as the nun had suggested.

Mother was truly concerned that I might be going blind. My vision was practically zero. The exam showed that I was extremely far-sighted, and the doctor told Mother my pupils had shrunk. He put drops in my eyes to dilate them, which made my vision even worse. I had to wear dark glasses for several days, but I didn't care because for the first time in my life, I had my mother to myself. She read to me and hugged me often. I never will forget that rare episode because it was the only time I was totally alone with Mother. When she took me back to the convent, it was one of the saddest days of my life.

It took another week before I was fitted with a pair of glasses. All that time, I was like a blind person. When I finally received the glasses, they were as thick as the bottom of a bottle and made my eyes look huge. I had no idea how magnified this made my eyes appear and how funny I looked. All I cared about was that I could see again. I couldn't wait to return to the convent, so I could show off my new glasses.

When I got back to the convent, much to my surprise, I was welcomed with disdain. Even my friends pointed fingers at me and laughed like I was some kind of a freak. Worse still, they began calling me "four eyes." I was mortified and deeply hurt. I could not understand why wearing glasses, which helped me see, could change the way my friends treated me. The taunting and ridicule I was subjected to every day was extremely hurtful, and it made me self-conscious throughout my childhood years. Not a day went by that someone did not make fun of me. No matter what class I was in, I was picked on and made fun of. The boys especially taunted me with unkind comments. My self-esteem was shattered. I developed an inferiority complex and became extremely shy, making me withdraw even more and seek the solace of my sketchpad and my secret guardian, who became my confidant.

The following year brought a severe flood. The rains came in unceasing torrents, causing the Merrimack River to overshoot its banks and nearly wipe out the downtown area. The convent was far enough away that it didn't cause any damage to our building, but the flood was said to be the worst our city had experienced in many years. The high winds and the pounding rain broke several windows, and the lone tree on the other side of the fence suffered broken limbs while the howling wind created havoc. The nuns ran around the rooms throwing Holy water at all the windows and pulling down all the green canvas shades to keep the lightning from coming into the rooms. We girls were told to sit on the floor in a circle and hold hands while we prayed to Saint Joseph, the protector of homes all night. We did not go to bed that night because it was too scary.

Another year, we were hit by the most severe hurricane ever recorded in New Hampshire. The wind blew so hard that we could feel the building shake. All the girls had been moved to the community room for safety reasons, and without exception, we were hysterical. We screamed with every burst of thunder, and I know we made as much noise as the hurricane outside. No amount of reassurance from the nuns or the older girls could convince us the building was not going to be blown away. We could see that the nuns were as frightened as we were, but they tried hard to convince us we were safe. They kept repeating, "Don't worry. God will protect us. He will not let the storm harm us."

They and the older girls went around with Holy water, blessing everything in sight. We sang hymns and prayed all night, as the wind blew with unbelievable force and the thunder boomed all around us. Lightning struck the huge, lone tree just on the other side of the fence, and it caught on fire. Luckily, it was raining so hard that the rain put the fire out before catching our fence on fire as well. Sometime in the wee hours of the morning, the storm finally abated and we all fell asleep on the floor.

The next morning, when all was calm once again, we were allowed to go outside to see what damage had been done. We could see only the mess that had taken place over our fence. We all immediately noticed that the beautiful tree that had been our only source of greenery was gone forever. The townspeople talked about the big hurricane of 1938 for years because it was the biggest catastrophe ever to hit New England. Little did we know at the time that over seven hundred people had died during that hurricane.

After the storms, life in the convent reverted to the same old routines. We took a bath only once each week. The rest of the time, we had to wash ourselves as best we could under our nightgowns while standing at the big sinks. Bath night was usually on a Saturday. Since there were so many girls, we had to take baths in shifts of ten. Two nuns prepared the bathroom, with its one lone bathtub. Hot water was scarce, as it had to be boiled in the kitchen on the first floor and brought up to the second floor in big buckets to fill the tub.

The tub was filled only once for each group of ten girls. When it was our turn to have a bath, we got in line and prayed that we would be one of the first because the first two girls got clean water and dry sheets. The sheet had a hole cut in the center to put the head through; this way, we were covered in back as well as in front. The first two girls sat in the tub back to back, with two nuns in attendance, one for each girl. Placing their hands under the sheet, they washed us. We were not allowed to wash ourselves. It was forbidden to touch our own bodies . . . especially our private areas. After a quick scrubbing, the nun dried us off as best she could as we slipped behind a big towel she held up, with her head turned to the side so she could not glimpse our exposed bodies. We then had to put on our nightgowns while she still held the towel between us. We were then instructed to brush our teeth and go to bed.

The next two girls were called in, and the entire process would begin all over. Subsequently, the same wet sheets would be put over the next girl's head. Having those wet cold sheets put over our body was always a shock, especially during the winter months. We would shiver and couldn't get warm even after being in bed awhile. The further down the line you were, the colder the sheets became, and the dirtier the water. Clean water and dry sheets were not provided until the next group of ten was called up. By the time the last two girls were called in, it would be past ten o'clock at night and nobody would be asleep because of the noise.

When I was around ten years old, Grandmother made Theresa and me identical dresses from a fabric of small green and white checks. Since we wore our convent uniforms most of the time, those dresses were special and worn only on rare occasions. One particular evening during the bathroom ritual that took place in the basement adjacent to the kitchen, Theresa and I were sent to the end of the line—the place reserved for the girls who were being punished. When the first girls got to the top of the stairs, they turned the lights out and left us in total darkness.

As we approached the bottom step parallel with the kitchen door, Theresa and I saw something simultaneously. It was a huge white hand floating around in the kitchen area, coming towards the door next to where we were standing. We both began screaming and pushing the girls in front of us, trying frantically to go up the stairs to get away from the hand that was coming towards us. The girls started falling as we pushed them in our hectic scramble to get up the stairs. Everyone started screaming, not knowing what was happening. Some girls became hysterical. It was total bedlam. When Theresa and I finally reached the top of the stairs, the nun ordered us to go back down. We tried to explain about the hand, but she said it was in our imagination, adding she knew it must be the devil trying to punish us for being disruptive and always getting into trouble. Theresa and I got back in line and walked up the stairs, holding hands in the dark. We eventually got to the top of the stairs. A short walk across the first floor hallway led to the second flight of stairs. As we approached the bottom step parallel with the luggage room to our left, the door of the luggage room flew open, and out jumped what appeared to be a devil wearing one of our green-and-white-checkered dresses. The snarling, hideous face had two horns protruding from the top of its head! It lunged at us, calling out our names in a guttural sound, "Lucille! Theresa!"

The devil tried to grab us! There was no stopping us now. I bolted up the stairs screaming, and ran to my bed with Theresa right behind me. My bed was next to the window of the fire escape stairway, and when I looked through the window, I saw the same big white hand! I flung myself under the bed and grabbed the springs under the mattress, jammed my feet under the springs, as well as my hands, pushing them as far as my arms would reach and holding on as tight as I could. I did not want to touch the floor with my body, for fear the devil would grab me. I screamed my head off in sheer panic. A nun tried to pull me away, but she couldn't reach me. She then ordered one of the older girls to try to pry my hands and feet from the springs, but she couldn't either. My fear gave me strength I did not know I had. I was convinced that if I let go, the devil would get me and carry me away. Poor Theresa was as hysterical as I was. We both stayed under our beds most of the night, clinging to the springs, afraid to let go and crying the entire time.

After that experience, Theresa and I were afraid of everything and especially afraid of the dark for many years. It left me more nervous than before. I shook when I was around strangers, and I began biting my nails. Sadly, it left Theresa permanently scarred. She lost all her self-confidence and became a victim of life. We feared the unknown after that, and worse still, we became pawns to be manipulated by anyone in a position of authority. My saving grace was the nightly contact with my spiritual guardian, whom I relied on mainly for solace.

5

FREEDOM

In 1937 Mother began dating a wonderful man named Arthur. She met him at one of the French clubs in town during a special event. From the onset, he began coming every Sunday with Mother to see Theresa and me. The first time I met him, I took a liking to him instantly because he was so much fun. Best of all, he treated me as if I were his daughter. For the first time in my life, I felt I had a father figure.

Arthur sold cars and had access to a car every day. Since we had never gone any place of consequence before, Sunday became a day I looked forward to because Arthur would take us to different places in what I considered his magical cars. Those excursions opened up the world to me, and as we traveled, I began to see life with a new perspective. We never knew which car he would appear in because he had a different one each time. Being a good salesman, he sold them fast! Our Sundays were now filled with anticipation, and I wondered what new thrills awaited me.

Arthur resembled Spencer Tracy, the movie star. He was about 5'10" tall, but to me he looked like a giant because I was so small. He had a deep dimple in his chin that got deeper when he smiled, and his blue-gray eyes sparkled all the time, giving him a delightful impish look that was impossible to resist. He also had a fantastic sense of humor, and was always kidding and making us laugh all the time. I trusted and admired him so much that I began copying his mannerisms. I wanted to be like him in every way.

I sensed that Arthur liked me because he made me feel special and he accepted me as I was, with my thick glasses and stringy hair. He was the first person in my life other than a relative who made me feel like a human being, not a freak. He showed me what true acceptance was. Even though Arthur spoke French, he insisted we speak English around him, stressing that English was the national language and it was important for us to be fluent in. It would help us when we got older.

Every Sunday, he drove us to the beaches around the endless coastlines of Maine, Massachusetts, and New Hampshire. I especially loved walking barefoot along the beach and feeling the water and sand squish between my toes. Some Sundays, he simply took us on long drives like to the White Mountains. The Old Man of the Mountain that nature had carved out of a huge boulder was a spectacular site I will never forget. He also drove us to many beautiful lakes and rivers that the area is known for. I did not realize at the time that one day I would recall these sites on canvas in my work as an artist.

Quite a few Sundays, we went to Fall River, Massachusetts, to visit two of Mother's favorite cousins, Rose and Claire. They were sisters who never married and lived together. Mother had not seen them for many years because they lived so far away, but now with access to a car, we visited them frequently.

On one of our visits, when I was around ten years old, Rose, Claire, Mother, and Arthur were sitting at the kitchen table drinking fresh brewed tea. Quite unexpectedly, I said, "Give me your cups when you finish and let me read your fortunes!"

That surprised all of them, but to go along with a child's whim, each one gave me their cup when they finished drinking their tea. Using one cup at a time, I slowly swirled the tea leaves in the cup, and after letting them settle in a natural pattern at the bottom, I told them what I saw. Evidently, I must have told them things that had already happened and events I saw in the tea leaves that foretold what would happen in the future. This was the first time I had done this, and frankly, I have no idea what made me say those things or why. It was a spontaneous inclination that was so natural; it felt as if I had done this many times before.

For many years, Mother reminded me of that episode, and whenever I saw Rose and Claire, they would remind me too. They were still in awe over my predictions and talked about them at great length with their friends.

Later on, they told me how amazed they were when some of the things I had predicted actually happened. Unfortunately, because I lived in the convent, the nuns had convinced me that I was possessed by the devil; therefore, I was afraid to pursue this psychic gift any further.

For several more years, the relief program continued to help Mother, so the state could pay for our stay in the convent. Our clothes, underwear, coats, and shoes all came from the welfare warehouses. People could always spot the children who were on welfare by the ugly clothes they wore. The older we became, the more embarrassed we were to be seen wearing clothes from the relief warehouse, especially when the other children made fun of us. Thank goodness, Grandmother made the dresses we wore outside of the convent.

In 1939 Mother was able to afford to move into her own apartment, located above a drug store within walking distance of the convent. It had three bedrooms and an immense kitchen, where we spent most of our time. Off the kitchen was a room we called the shed that really served as a pantry and storage room. It led out to a pebbled roof, which became our first patio and a place for us to play outdoors. For the next eight months after Mother moved, whenever it was cold or raining, we would spend that Sunday visiting in her apartment instead of going for a ride. That summer, rather than going to Aunt Delia's farm for two months, we began staying in the apartment instead. My life began to change drastically, and having lived in a regimented environment for so many years, I did not like it. I found it hard to accept change.

One glorious Sunday in 1940, Theresa and I left the convent for the last time. I could not believe it when Mother told us the good news. I was twelve years old at the time, and we had been in the convent eight years under dictatorial control. The thought of living with our brother for the first time in our lives was the most wonderful news I could imagine. We were going to be a family at last.

The first week in my new home took some adjusting. The contrast between my former regimented lifestyle and the freedom I now enjoyed seemed like heaven. Mother was strict, but in a loving, caring way. It made me want to do whatever she ordered. One of the rules she imposed was that we were not permitted to leave the house without her permission. The other rule was that we were not allowed to have friends over unless she was at home.

Within a few weeks, my brother Emile moved in with us. To have our family together for the first time after so many years apart was unbelievable. After a few days, though, we discovered that Emile, now eleven years old, presented a bit of a problem. His habits, as well as his likes and dislikes, were totally different from ours. Having lived with relatives who doted on him made him think he could have his way all the time. He was a handful for Mother to control in the beginning, and it took weeks for him to adjust to his expectations not being fulfilled.

Mother was overwhelmed at times with three children, all nearly teenagers with different temperaments. It required a great deal of patience and adjustments on her part, I'm sure. It was a trying time for all of us, until we eventually learned what most families become accustomed to after living together for many years. We were forced to learn to give and take, and within two months, we learned how to become a happy household.

For the first time in my life, I started to have some unstructured time just for myself. One of the joys this new freedom allowed me was time to pursue my passion for drawing and coloring. I remember looking forward to the rainy days, so I would be left undisturbed in my room, free to experiment and draw to my heart's content. I became so absorbed in what I was doing that the hours flew by. I went into my subconscious and recalled the beautiful scenes I had seen on the many Sunday drives. My passion became fixed on capturing the variety of trees, the unusual cloud formations, and the reflections in the lakes and ponds. Capturing their beauty from memory was a thrilling challenge.

When fall arrived, Mother enrolled Theresa and me in a French junior high school that was walking distance from where we lived. Thank goodness, the nuns who taught there were of a different order than the ones we'd had in the convent. Being twelve years old, walking home after school for the first time in my life was a thrill beyond words.

Theresa and I still did not speak English very well, and Emile, who had always attended public schools, spoke only English. This created a problem in our house. I decided to speak only English from now on, and in three months time, my English was as good as Emile's. I'm sure this helped cement my relationship with my brother. Emile and I discovered that we had much in common and became close buddies. I preferred playing with him and his friends for a long time.

When Theresa turned thirteen, we drifted apart. It was strange how she and I no longer had anything in common. In fact, we constantly held the opposite view on just about any given subject. What added to our differences was the whispering that had gone on in the older girls' dorm room in the convent was now taking place in our home between Theresa and her friends. I was an outcast.

The next few years were mainly carefree. I was more interested in going to the movies, which provided a great escape from the dull life I led. Movies and documentaries were my introduction to world events, making me aware of the war taking place in Europe. With Hitler bombing and capturing the countries that fell under his conquests, Germany became a threat to the world. I was only thirteen and did not understand the significance of what was going on, but I remember the uneasy feeling I experienced as I watched those terrible events projected on the screen.

Mother moved to another apartment in 1941, closer to the school we attended and in the same building that my grandmother lived in. Our new neighborhood was more residential, quiet, and much cleaner. The new area gave me the opportunity to meet new friends, and it changed my life. Within a few months, I celebrated my thirteenth birthday. I now understood what my older sister and her friends had been giggling and whispering about for the past two years. I was growing up and becoming a young lady.

My new best friend, Irene, and I became inseparable. She was a beauty with huge blue eyes and long curly auburn hair. I admired her self-confidence and wished I could be more like her. We shared a love for music and soon developed a love for dancing. The big bands came to our town every Saturday night and Irene, Theresa, and I became regulars. We practiced dancing with each other until we were excellent at doing the jitterbug. We became known as some of the best dancers in town. When Saturday night arrived, we walked to the dance hall and mingled with the other girls while waiting for one of the boys to ask us to dance. Inevitably, the boys flocked to Irene; she never missed a dance. In the beginning, I was seldom asked to dance. I knew it was because I wore thick glasses, no makeup, was skinny, and had not yet developed breasts.

This all changed when Irene asked me to come along to visit a friend of hers one Sunday afternoon. The girl lived in another part of town, so we had to ride a bus for the first time. Buses had been introduced to our town the year before, replacing all the trolley cars that we had become accustomed to.

I was surprised when I met Irene's friend, Jacqueline. She was striking and every bit as pretty as Irene. She was also sophisticated beyond her years. At seventeen, she could easily have passed for a twenty year old. She lived in New York City and had come to visit her parents to celebrate her eighteenth birthday in a few weeks. Being of legal age when she returned to New York, she would be able to fulfill her dream of becoming a model for a top fashion house. After we became better acquainted, she asked if I minded if she experimented with my hair, saying she enjoyed trying different hairstyles just for fun. It was a hobby she practiced with some of the other models in New York. My hair had no luster, was as straight as a pencil, and was really unattractive. I told her to please do whatever she wanted. She washed my hair with a wonderful-smelling shampoo, dried it, and for the first time in my life, my hair had a lovely shine. She began trying different styles and decided on an upsweep—the current fad of the day. Jacqueline was pleased with the results and began applying pancake makeup and lipstick to my face. Like a sculptor, she examined me carefully and said she was pleased with her work. When she finished, she told me to go in her bathroom and look at myself in the mirror without my glasses. The transformation made me look like a stranger. The change was so complete that I could hardly believe the person in the mirror was really me. After thanking Jacqueline a million times, Irene and I left.

Strange how people come into our lives at certain times, just when we need them. The encounter was totally unexpected and made a huge impact on my life. As we rode the bus back home, some of the passengers stared at me. Several men even smiled and winked. I decided that day that from now on, I would wear my glasses only in the classroom. My unseen guardian flashed in my mind, making me wonder if he had led me to this wonderful experience in order to boost my self-esteem.

Returning home, Mother was shocked when she saw me. Seeing her thirteen-year-old child looking like a seventeen-year-old was disturbing to say the least. One look at me, and she shouted, "Go wash your face! You are too young to wear makeup, and that hairstyle makes you look too grown-up. Don't ever let me see you wearing makeup again until you are at least sixteen years old! Do I make myself clear, young lady?"

Rather than start an argument, I did as I was told but decided I would carry lipstick in my pocket. Whenever I left the house, I would put some on, making sure that I took it off before I returned home. I could not believe how my new appearance made people friendlier towards me. Even the boys were nicer. Within a few months, I became as popular as Irene, and boys began asking me to dance. I learned that beautiful people create an aura that attracts others, and I was ready to experience the world from this newly discovered vantage point.

Being the era of the jitterbug, the girls who were really "with-it" wore short pleated skirts above the knee, with long blazer jackets within about two inches above the skirt. That fashion was considered pretty daring in those days. Theresa and I loved to dance the jitterbug and dressed in the fashion of the times. I had a burgundy corduroy jacket with big shoulder pads that I wore with my skirts. I probably owned no more than two skirts, but since it was a fad to borrow clothes from our friends, we all enjoyed the benefit of a much larger wardrobe. The boys wore outfits called "zoot suits."

That same year, I was a freshman in high school. My favorite subject was English, and I especially enjoyed writing poems and book reports. My teacher, Miss Sullivan, encouraged me to write what I felt and instilled a love of writing in me. I don't think she knew that on some of my book reports, I read only the beginning of the book, some pages in the middle, and a few pages at the end. I studied the pictures to make sure I had the names right, then I made up my own interpretation of the story. Much to my delight, I usually made A's. I enjoyed school and learned quickly.

6

TRAUMA AND DOUBTS

As much as my life was changing, the world was changing more. We were going through a horrific transformation. News about Hitler and his regime's destruction of Europe bombarded use from the radio as well as at the movie theater on Saturdays. It was disturbing to hear, but honestly, being a teenager, I did not understand the seriousness of what was happening. It seemed so remote that I felt it didn't affect me. I was more concerned about having as much fun as possible.

I distinctly remember the day all that changed. I had gone to the movies with my sister and some friends. While we were enjoying the cartoons, the lights came on and the screen went black. The owner of the theater came running down the aisle, and with a quivering voice announced, "Everybody go home immediately! The theatre is closed. The Japanese have bombed Pearl Harbor, and President Roosevelt has declared war on the Japanese!"

It was a day I will never forget—December 7, 1941. A silence fell over the crowd as his words sunk in. The cacophony of everyone talking at once became deafening as we made a mad dash for the doors. I rushed home, frightened beyond words at the news I had just heard. A terrible feeling of foreboding made me wonder what being at war was going to be like.

Mother was already at home in a state of panic and crying uncontrollably. She told us the factories had let the people go home early after hearing the news on the radio. She was worried that her brother, Uncle Oliver, would be required to join the army. Already, the news announcer on the radio was saying all men eighteen years old and up were being drafted and told to report to the nearest army base immediately. Those who did not want to be in the army could enlist in the navy, merchant marines, marine corps, or army air corps.

Mother tried to explain what a war would be like and how much our lives would change. As the weeks went by, people were asked to donate whatever aluminum pots and pans they had in their possession to help the war effort. I remember Mother giving away all but one of her pots. Aluminum was badly needed for building ships, planes, and other equipment to prepare America for the war. Later, Mother bought stainless steel pots and pans to replace the ones she had donated.

Many factories were built from scratch. Others that had manufactured basic goods were now expanding to produce the demands for war-related products. Even the textile mills were converted to manufacture soldiers' uniforms, underwear, and stockings. Shoe factories went into full gear, making boots and other types of military foot wear. Nylon factories made parachutes instead of nylons for women.

Not long after entering the war with Japan, the United States became involved with the war in Europe. Our American boys were sent to help our allies in England, France, and other nations that the Germans were invading. It was a most confusing, frightening time in the United States, dismantling our way of life.

Factories stayed open day and night to keep up with the workload, and the shortage of male workers created a demand for women. To entice workers to work at night, factories paid time and a half for overtime. The night shift was dubbed the "swing shift." Women began going to work in droves, starting at age sixteen. At long last, World War II put an end to the Depression.

Once again, we found that out of a horrible situation, some good does come. We also found out that Mother had been right the day she first heard the news that we were entering the war to fear what could happen. Uncle Oliver was drafted into the army as a field cook, and after his basic training, he was sent to a Philippine island called Luzon.

Mother's boyfriend Arthur had been declared 4F because of a physical problem and could not enlist, nor could he be drafted. He seized the opportunity to start making more money and moved to Connecticut.

Some months later, the area he moved to became a Mecca for factories that manufactured airplane parts. As a floor manager, he made excellent wages. Once he was comfortably settled into a rental house, he convinced Mother to visit him, and after a few months of repeated visits, persuaded her to apply for a job at one of the ball-bearing manufacturing plants.

There was such a great demand for workers that Mother was hired immediately. A few weeks later, she moved to Connecticut, but before leaving, she arranged to have Grandmother live with us while she was away. I overheard her telling Grandmother one morning that the salary she would make was more than she had made in a year during all of her previous jobs. As soon as school ended in June, we helped pack our belongings and drove to New Britain, Connecticut, in Arthur's car.

In the meantime, Arthur found Mother an apartment that was conveniently located behind his house. All we had to do was walk across the backyard, and we'd be at his house in less than a minute. During the war years, apartments were very scarce, so people took whatever they could find. Our apartment was on the first floor of a three-story building with two apartments on each floor. We had three small bedrooms and a kitchen. Unfortunately, not every apartment had a bathroom. We were forced to share a toilet in the hall with a family that had five children.

The mother of that family was lazy, and her husband happened to be a musician who was on the road performing with his band all the time. Therefore, he seldom came home. The few times I had to visit with her, I noticed that the beds were not made, the clothes were strewn all over the place, and the sink was full of dirty dishes. This lifestyle created an infestation of cockroaches throughout the building. I have no idea how the other tenants coped with the problem; all I know is, even though we kept our apartment spotless, it was impossible to keep the roaches out of our connecting side. Mother used bug-killing powder daily, but we still had roaches in our apartment every day.

Having to share a toilet in the hall with that family became a nightmare. The bathroom was the width of the stairwell, about four feet square. It could only accommodate a toilet with a tank mounted on the wall and a pull chain to flush it. Each time we had to use the bathroom, we had to bring along our own toilet paper. When we used the toilet at night, as soon as we turned the light on, roaches crawled across the walls and scurried across the ceiling. Many times, they fell on me if I didn't hurry. How I envied my brother's outdoor plumbing because he could sneak outside at night and relieve himself behind the house. I even tried that myself a few times, but having to keep a watchful eye while in a squatting position proved too precarious. I decided it was less risky to deal with the roaches.

One night, I entered the toilet expecting to relieve myself quickly and did not turn the light on. After sitting down, I heard splashing in the toilet bowl. I jumped up, turned the light on, and discovered that a rat had fallen into the bowl. I ran out screaming.

The bedroom Theresa and I slept in was so small that Mother had to buy bunk beds. I had the top bunk because Theresa was the oldest and had first choice. My brother Emile slept on a cot on the opposite wall. There was barely enough room to walk between the beds. With this cramped situation, the only time we went to our bedroom was to sleep.

During the winter months, a Franklin coal-burning heater in the kitchen provided our only source of heat for those harsh New England winters. Without a thermostat, Mother had to guess how much coal to put in it. Her solution was to fill the stove to the brim before going to bed. That way, she did not have to get up during the night. The temperature often reached over 100 degrees, making it unbearably hot on the top bunk. Many nights I thought I would suffocate. As a matter of fact, a chain for the overhead light in the kitchen had a glass ball attached at the end of it with wax inside the ball. One night the heat got so intense that the glass ball shattered, and the wax melted onto the table below.

I'm surprised we didn't all die from carbon monoxide fumes.

I enrolled in the local public high school that same year. Having taken art courses at my previous high school, I wanted to continue to pursue my dream of becoming an artist. One day our assignment was to draw a maple leaf from memory. Having spent my childhood surrounded mostly by concrete, I really did not have a mental image of what a maple leaf looked like. I went to the teacher and tried to explain that I did not know how to draw a maple leaf. With disdain, he told me to pick up my things, that I did not belong in his class. I was embarrassed and felt my dream had come to an end. When the bell rang, I bolted out of there and never went back. I put my quest for becoming an artist on hold for many years.

I changed to a home economics class. That was an unexpected blessing because I learned skills that helped me during my entire life. When school ended the following year, I had completed my junior year. A few weeks later, I turned sixteen. Mother believed girls did not need to be in school past sixteen and insisted that I apply for a job where she worked. The majority of parents in those days believed that girls did not need to go to school past the eighth grade. They encouraged them to get married and have their husbands provide for them. I did not regret leaving school, even though I lacked only one year to graduate. Up to that point, I was proud because I had attended school longer than any other female in our family. I applied for a job and was hired right away, since they were so desperate for workers. I enjoyed working because it presented a challenge for me and I could use my imagination.

* * *

Being sixteen, my outlook on life changed. I wanted to seek answers to the many questions that had been forming in my mind. I had doubts about God, in fact, about religion in general. I suggested to Theresa that we skip church one Sunday and go to a restaurant instead. Not wanting Mother to suspect anything, we dressed in our usual Sunday finery. We walked to a restaurant outside our neighborhood to avoid being seen by someone we might know. After ordering coffee, I looked around, feeling uncomfortable that we were doing something wrong. When we ordered our second cup of coffee, I realized nobody had paid attention to us, so I relaxed. We stayed until we were sure the service was over, and then we casually joined the rest of the people who were on their way home after attending church.

While getting ready for lunch, Mother asked me what the sermon was about. Without hesitating, I made up a story, using one of the sermons I had heard in the past. This went over so well that Theresa and I decided to skip church again the following Sunday. After a while, we stopped going to church altogether, and instead, we looked forward to spending that hour on Sunday morning with friends at our favorite café.

It did not occur to me at the time that I had lied to my Mother. I just decided I'd had my fill of religion. Many adults I knew went to church religiously every Sunday, yet I knew they were hypocrites. I began remembering the abuse I had endured in the convent. Was that what religion was supposed to be like? I suppose I had reached the age of reasoning and needed to search for the meaning of life.

The more I thought about it, the more it made no sense to me. I began questioning the logic and truth about what I had been told all my life. I figured if God really existed, he would eventually show himself to me. In the meantime, I decided to live my life carefree and just have a good time.

7

MEETING ERNIE

In 1944 the United States was seriously at war with Japan. Although casualties and deaths were mounting, patriotism was at an all-time high. Young men still flocked to join the military because they were proud to serve their country. The fighting escalated in the jungles of the Pacific, especially on islands we had never heard of before, such as Luzon, Iwo Jima, and the Howland Islands (where Amelia Earhart presumably crashed her plane). They were overrun by elusive Japanese soldiers whose main mission was to kill the American soldiers. To add to the slaughter, the freezing terrain in Europe and the sweltering desert heat of Africa claimed countless other lives. The soldiers who were fortunate enough to come home on leave talked their girlfriends into getting married. Young couples reasoned that it might be the last time they would be together before he was sent off to fight. So many young girls decided to get married, that it was almost like an epidemic.

It truly was a time for romance, and I wanted my share of this rapture. Having been influenced by the many romantic movies I had seen, I longed for a Prince Charming to come into my life. I expected a hero who would rescue me from my poor existence, believing he would fulfill my every need and love me forever.

After working all week at the factory, I looked forward to Saturday night, when I could abandon my cares to the beat and sounds of the latest dance music. My girlfriends and I would catch the bus that went to the dance complex located on the outskirts of Hartford.

The immense dance pavilion with a grand ballroom that accommodated well over one hundred people was nestled in a beautiful park setting. Every weekend, one of the nation's most popular big bands played as we danced our cares away.

One Saturday, I was especially excited because Artie Shaw was the featured band playing that night. After dancing over an hour, I felt extremely hot and decided to go outside to sit by the lake and cool off. As I walked, a refreshing breeze caressed my burning cheeks, and I was drawn to a bench that faced the water. The bright full moon cast a huge light beam in the center of the water, and the wind created ripples that made it look like diamonds dancing on the surface. I sat there staring at the incredible view and entered into one of my trance-like states. That old familiar feeling of being transported in time engulfed me. My surroundings disappeared, and my thoughts floated to another dimension.

Then, like a thunderclap, a man's voice behind me was saying, "Don't move!" It broke my spell.

I was startled out of my deep trance and carefully looked behind me to see who the intruder was. Standing to my left was a young man in an army uniform. He had his fingers shaped like someone taking a picture, focusing on my face the way an artist does to capture just the right angle of his subject. Then he spoke again. "I don't want you to move. I want to remember this scene with you in silhouette, with the moon reflected on the water behind you. It is the most incredible sight I have ever seen."

I was annoyed and not the least bit impressed. Not only had he scared me but also his outburst had ruined a wonderful moment, an experience one cannot recapture at will.

I angrily responded, "Are you in the habit of scaring girls? You don't impress me with your flattery!"

He quickly apologized, saying, "I'm sorry if I frightened you, but you have no idea how overcome I was when I spotted you in this setting. I never would have been able to recapture the moment if you had moved."

Unexpectedly, he sat down on the bench next to me, and while extending his right hand, he introduced himself, saying, "Hi, I'm Ernie Cafege." He went on to say he was twenty-six years old and was a Master Sergeant in the Army Medical Corps. He told me he was newly stationed at Avon, a small town near Hartford. The Army Medical Corps had taken over an all-boys' academy, formally a preparatory school, and had converted it to a rehabilitation center for soldiers who were blinded in battle.

His smile calmed me and made me relax, and I began enjoying our conversation. Ernie was not tall. I estimated about five feet six inches, but he certainly looked impressive in his uniform. His interesting wide-set eyes were dark brown with specks of yellow. They were different from any I had seen, and his chestnut-colored hair had traces of blond streaks running through it. Actually, he was not bad looking, but he did not fit my idea of handsome, nor did he strike me as a Prince Charming. Yet, I found him interesting.

We talked until we noticed that the music had stopped, and many dancers were flocking outside to get into their cars. Others were boarding the waiting buses.

With everyone talking at once, the moment was energized with excitement. Not wanting to leave my side, Ernie asked if he could sit next to me on the bus, adding he had to go to Hartford to catch another bus going to Avon. My mood became reckless, and without much thought, I told him it was fine with me.

At this point, I was feeling adventurous and never expected we would see each other again. We boarded the bus and took seats in the back next to my sister and her friend Veronica. Two soldiers who were also stationed at Avon accompanied them. After the introductions, we began a nonstop conversation until we reached our destination. When we got off the bus in Hartford, instead of transferring to our buses as previously planned, we opted to go to a restaurant for a late snack instead. The stimulating topics we discussed and the endless laughter kept us glued to our seats until three o'clock in the morning. By the time we realized how late it was, we had to hurry to catch the last buses going to our separate destinations.

Being with an older man was a new experience for me. Up until then, I had dated only boys my own age or slightly older. Even though Ernie was nine years older than me, I felt comfortable in his presence, and frankly, did not notice any difference. I was captivated and a bit smitten by all the attention he lavished on me. He asked for my address, and before boarding my bus, I gave it to him because at the time, we did not have a telephone.

The following Wednesday, while Mother was preparing dinner, I was surprised by a knock at the door. Being close by, I opened it to find Ernie standing there with a sheepish grin. He said, "I took the chance that you would be home because I haven't been able to get you out of my mind since we met. I did not want to wait until next Saturday to see you again."

After asking him to come in, I introduced him to my mother and Emile. I had talked about him so much that they felt like they already knew him. Theresa, whom we now called Terry, was teasing me in the background, feeling smug because she already knew him. I could tell that Mother took a liking to him when she invited him to stay for dinner.

After dinner, Ernie and I went for a long walk and resumed our never-ending conversation about all sorts of subjects, but mainly about my love of poetry. After a while, Ernie suggested we continue our talk in my favorite café. Over coffee and custard pie, he quoted several poems. I listened to him recite poems from the *Rubaiyat of Omar Khayyam* from memory. The words had a familiar, magical sound, as if I had heard them before. I wanted to hear more and was surprised to learn that Ernie knew most of the one hundred and one quatrains by heart. I was extremely impressed.

As we walked back to my house, I felt as if my feet were floating on the pavement while my mind was still trying to absorb all the things I had just heard. By the time he took me back home, it was late and Ernie had to hurry to catch the bus going to Hartford. As we said goodnight, I sensed this was the start of something beyond my control.

Sure enough, after that night, Ernie began sending me love letters and postcards. The following week, he surprised me again on Wednesday night and stayed for dinner. We spent several hours over coffee in the café, establishing a new routine. On the way back to my house, he told me he also wanted to visit me on Sundays from now on.

After four weeks of these visits, he presented me with a package. I was not used to receiving presents and was totally surprised. My face flushed as all eyes fell on me.

I carefully removed the paper, and to my profound joy, discovered it was a book: The *Rubaiyat of Omar Kayyam*. It was my very first book. My profound love of books was established that very day. Seeing the beautifully illustrated edition was overwhelming, and I began to cry. For the first time in my young life, a thoughtful gift moved me to tears.

The following month, Mother consented to let me go to Avon on a Sunday to visit Ernie. She insisted that Terry go with me as my chaperone. Terry had been seeing Bob, the soldier she had met at the dance the night I met Ernie. Since they did not have much in common, their time together had not developed into more than a close friendship.

As we rode the bus to Hartford that beautiful summer day, Terry and I could not have been happier. We transferred to the bus going to Avon without a problem and arrived by late morning. I had never been that far from home without my mother before, and I must admit I was frightened. I feared we might get lost, or worse, not find the bus that would take us back home. Having spent my childhood under strict control, the unknown was a menacing threat to me.

Avon reminded me of the boys' schools in some of the old English movies I had seen. The varied buildings were made of gray and white stones resembling old forts. The main entrance was gated with a guardhouse. The campus had a central courtyard, and the well-manicured grounds extended for many miles. Terry and I were stopped at the gate, and the guard asked us our names, plus the names of the soldiers we had come to visit. Being a military complex, security was high. We waited fifteen minutes while they processed our passes, and in no time at all, Ernie and Bob came for us. They exchanged plans as to where and when we would meet later, then Ernie and I left to go exploring on our own.

Once we crossed the courtyard, he led me into a chapel, where he wanted to show me something of importance. We seated ourselves in the center of the room, and in a whisper he said, "I want you to be very quiet; try not to make a sound."

Barely a minute went by when I heard the door open. Ernie put his finger to his mouth, indicating for me not to say a word. Then a man's voice bellowed, "Who's here?"

We both stayed very still, and the man repeated, "Who's here? I know someone is in this room. Please, say something."

Ernie finally responded, "It's me, Ernie. I have my girlfriend with me."

We got up and went over to where the man was standing. As we approached him, I noticed from his facial movements that he was blind. Ernie introduced me to Mark, and we exchanged greetings. Sheepishly Mark said, "May I touch your face? I want to see what you look like. I haven't been near a woman in over a year, and to feel a woman's skin would give me the greatest pleasure."

"Of course," I said, and Mark approached me in silence with a look of reverence on his face, as if he was going to inspect a great work of art. With his fingertips, he began to gently examine my face. He started with my cheeks, then my nose and onto my forehead. He stroked my eyelids, my hair, then my cheeks and neck. His touch was as soft as a feather flittering across my face. With tears in his eyes, he said, "Ernie, you old devil. You are right. She is even more beautiful than you described."

Ernie laughed and slapped him on the back to break the tension, then added, "Come on, you two. Let's go get something to eat. I'm sure Lucille is hungry after that long bus ride."

Over lunch, I learned that Ernie was the physical education instructor for all of the blind GIs at Avon. He taught them acrobatics, bowling, swimming, horseback riding, whatever other sport they wanted to learn. It was a new program that Ernie helped establish for the army. Mark and all the other men who came by our table spoke highly of Ernie. They said he had given them courage and faith in their new abilities by teaching them activities that would help them in their new life. It helped them regain the self-confidence that many had lost. It was sad to learn that many feared going back home to their families or sweethearts. Not knowing how they would react to their blindness was the most fearful part of all, Mark said.

After lunch, Mark left us to go join his other buddies. Ernie seized the opportunity to lead me for a stroll around the park-like grounds. We found an old elm tree, sat next to its massive trunk, and talked for an endless amount of time. My previous conversation with Mark and the other young men had consumed me with sadness, and I could not erase their faces from my mind. Seeing my changed mood, Ernie explained that the reason he wanted me to be quiet back in the chapel was so I could discover first hand that blind people can see with their fingertips. He explained it was a new discovery that had the medical field puzzled and excited. Even though the blind cannot see with their eyes, they can feel a person in a room because they have a heightened sense called facial vision, Ernie said. It is truly remarkable what a blind person can sense, Ernie marveled; they have a sixth sense that defies understanding. This revelation eased my mind somewhat, and I listened more attentively when he began telling me about himself.

Even though Ernie was small in stature, he had developed his body like all great athletes. The muscles in his arms and legs bulged because he had trained for years to be an expert tumbler and gymnast. His life-long ambition had been to compete in the Olympics some day. Unfortunately, when the war broke out, he was drafted into the army, and that put an end to his goal because when the war ended, he would be too old to compete.

He also loved to write and confided that his new goal was to become a journalist. Before dusk, and after a fabulous day in Avon, Terry and I said goodbye to Ernie and Bob and headed for our bus stop.

Reliving the events of the day, I felt a new excitement. At the time, I did not know the symptoms one experiences when falling in love. After that wonderful day, I continued going on dates with other boys because I liked to dance, and Ernie did not know how. I was not yet ready to give up my love of dancing for him. But, within a few months, I found boys around my age to be boring. My love of seeking knowledge became more important to me than even dancing had been.

Once again, I began experiencing thoughts that I had lived on earth before, and the recollection of past events made me wonder where those thoughts came from. The vivid awareness of knowing things before they happened began to resurface. It was like a nudge to remind me of the great gifts I had been born with and to begin meditating the way I once had.

I renewed my old habit of staring at a light source while lying in bed at night. I was reluctant to reveal these experiences to anyone because I was afraid they would laugh at me, or worse still, they would think I was crazy.

Once I made up my mind that I could trust Ernie, the next time we were together, I decided to tell him about my strange experiences. I made him promise not to tell my secret to another soul. Feeling confident that he would not betray me, I revealed the unusual episodes I'd had while in the convent. I explained the divine guidance I received during my form of meditation and the comfort I received from my spiritual guide during my most traumatic ordeals. Ernie smiled, and then told me he had read many books about the phenomenon I described. I was happy to learn that books were written about that very subject, and relieved to learn I was not the only one who had those experiences. He of course wanted to hear more detailed events, but my inner voice warned me to be cautious, and I divulged only a few things.

Our romance blossomed to a goodnight kiss, and holding hands was as physical as we got. Actually, I did not know there was any more to dating than that. Those were the days when girls were expected to be virgins when they married, and I was happy in my ignorance.

At this time, the war in Europe was ending and the war with Japan was still raging. Efforts to get the Japanese to surrender failed, and we entered another year. Suddenly, on April 12, 1945, President Franklin Delano Roosevelt died of a cerebral hemorrhage, sending the world into a state of shock. The great president who had guided us through the Depression was gone.

Vice President Harry Truman was quickly sworn in and assumed the responsibilities as our next president. After being in office only four months, he ordered the Enola Gay to drop the first atomic bomb on Hiroshima on August 6, 1945. The world was shocked by his decision, but that tragic bombing succeeded in bringing the Japanese to their senses and ended the war with Japan. World War II was finally over.

Soldiers were released from active duty on a priority system. Ernie received orders to report to a base in Cape Cod, Massachusetts, pending his discharge. As soon as he was settled on the base, I was able to visit him occasionally on weekends. Before long, we both realized it was harder to break away and say goodbye. Two months before my eighteenth birthday, Ernie asked me to marry him. Mother had to approve the marriage because I was underage, and she gladly did so.

Within a week, the three of us were on a train heading for Cleveland, Ohio, where Ernie's parents lived. He wanted his entire family to meet me, at long last. He wanted them to be included in the wedding ceremony. The wedding party consisted of Mr. and Mrs. Cafege, Ernie's three brothers, and his sister Catherine, who agreed to be my matron of honor.

It wasn't the grand wedding I had dreamed of having, but it was a memorable day just the same. The reception that followed with a banquet style meal at a downtown hotel rivaled any of my previous experiences. Regrettably, we had to postpone our honeymoon because Ernie had to return to his base within a few days. The next morning, we left to catch the afternoon train that was leaving for New Hampshire.

The train was packed with soldiers from every branch of the services returning home from the war zones. Some were with large families, others with sweethearts or wives. So many people were on the train that all the seats were taken. Many people, including the three of us, had to sit on luggage in the aisles. The congested aisles made it almost impossible for anyone to walk by. When a family of four seated next to us got up to transfer to another train, we quickly grabbed their seats. The wooden cane-backed bench seats were fairly comfortable, and I spent the time viewing the unforgettable countryside zipping by while holding hands with my new husband.

When we finally arrived at Mother's apartment, we were exhausted and dirty. We had slept as best we could while sitting up on those wooden seats. Now our backs and legs were screaming to be stretched out. Mother was kind enough to give us her bedroom.

The next morning Ernie had to leave to get back to his base on time. We clung to each other when we had to part at the bus station. Before leaving, he made me promise to look for an apartment as soon as possible. I spent two weeks looking, but there were none available in town. I decided to search the newspaper, and one day, an ad advertising for a nanny caught my eye. The job included room and board. I immediately called from a payphone, hoping no one else had called ahead of me. I was able to arrange an interview for the very next day.

My stomach was in knots as I dressed, and the nervous tension continued while I took the bus to the north end of town, where the rich people lived. After walking two blocks, I arrived at a long driveway that led to a big house with massive white pillars on the front porch. The magnificent house and the beautifully landscaped grounds made me feel ill at ease. I wondered if I was qualified for the position, and almost turned back, when in my mind I heard, "Go on, it will be all right." My ever-present spirit guide gave me the encouragement I needed. After taking a deep breath, I approached the front door and rang the bell. Before the person even answered the door, I knew instinctively that I would get the job. It was an intuitive knowing that was happening more frequently.

A charming woman came to the door and introduced herself as Mrs. Pease, the owner. I introduced myself and told her I had come for the job interview. Mrs. Pease was very attractive and not much older than me. She reminded me of the wealthy English ladies I had seen in the movies. Actually, she looked very much like Greer Garson, the movie star.

When we sat down for the interview, she called her two boys over to join us. Collin, the eldest, was four, and Bart was a two-year-old. She told them to come and meet the nice lady who might be their new nanny. Both of them had light blond hair and green eyes, just like their mother. Even though they were two years apart, they could easily have been twins, since Bart was nearly as tall as Collin. They were dressed and scrubbed to a shine, as if they were going to church. Her husband entered the room, and we were introduced.

Mr. Pease was a perfect specimen of a high-class gentleman. He appeared to be around twenty-eight years old, very tall, and slender. Frankly, I thought he was quite dashing in his gray pinstriped suit and the white starched shirt, enhanced the navy and gray silk tie he was wearing. I couldn't help but notice the stickpin in his tie that flashed a diamond the size of a large green pea. As we shook hands, I noticed that even his nails were manicured.

Mr. Pease was extremely polite and proceeded to tell me that they were from England. He told me he owned one of the defense plants in town and was gone a good part of the time. He had come home early that day to help his wife decide whom they should hire. Mrs. Pease served us tea while we continued to talk. Since it was Friday, Mrs. Pease asked if I could start working on Monday. I told her yes and left. I was so excited, I ran all the way to the bus stop.

On Saturday I went to work in the factory as usual and told my boss I would not be coming back, saying it would be one less person for him to lay off. He thanked me and wished me luck.

Early Sunday morning I called Ernie to tell him the good news. He was thrilled to learn I had found not only a job but also a position that would provide us private rooms in a magnificent house.

When I went to work on Monday, I brought a few of my clothes because I was actually moving in. I had arranged with Arthur to help me bring the rest of my belongings in his car the following Sunday—the only day I would have off.

Mrs. Pease greeted me like a long-lost sister. Collin and Bart clung to her while they followed us up the stairs to my new quarters. They jumped and carried on like two young puppies the entire time. Without warning, both boys wrapped their arms around my legs and begged me to pick them up. I had to tell them that I couldn't right then, but I would as soon as I could. That made them happy, and they ran off to play together.

When Mrs. Pease and I entered the room that was to be my new home, I was surprised to see it contained twin beds. They had identical massive antique headboards made of cherry wood that were exquisitely carved. The adjoining bathroom was the size of a bedroom, with everything that I never had before, including a bathtub.

I was told that my duty was to keep the boys occupied. I was to play with them, read to them, and take them for walks. I would feed them breakfast, lunch, and dinner, and would have to eat all my meals with them. After dinner, I was to give them a bath and read them stories until they fell asleep. Luckily, they had twin beds and shared the same room. The adjoining room was their playroom. It was filled with the latest toys, games, and books, all neatly arranged like a daycare center. Those boys had everything a child could possibly want.

My other duties included dusting the entire house, making sure the living room was always picked up, with no newspapers or magazines left on the floor. Clutter of any kind was not tolerated in any part of the house. My other job, however, was the most demanding. After the boys were put to bed, I had to help Mrs. Pease prepare their evening meal and serve it to them. While the food was cooking, I would set the table. Mrs. Pease would go to her room to freshen up, while Mr. Pease did the same. She would change into an elegant dress, and they would come down the stairs together. They sat at opposite ends of the long dining room table. Mrs. Pease had a buzzer by her right foot that she would press for me to bring in the first course. The next buzzer would mean to gather the dirty dishes and bring out the second course. In-between courses, the buzzer would summon me to refill their water glasses or their wine glasses. After the main meal was finished, I would be summoned to bring in the dessert. During their meal, I had to stay in the kitchen and wait for the sound of the buzzer. After I served them their traditional hot tea, Mrs. Pease would buzz twice. This was to let me know it was time to clear the table. By the time everything was put back in order, it would be close to eleven o'clock at night. On the nights they had guests for dinner, it would be well past midnight before I ventured up to my room.

After my first week, I wondered if I had made a terrible mistake. But as the weeks went by, I realized how much I was learning and developed a routine that made it all seem quite natural and pleasant. I rested and meditated while the boys took a nap in the afternoon, and I was refreshed and ready to tackle my next duties when they woke up.

As the weeks went by, Mrs. Pease and I developed a close friendship. Once in awhile, when the boys were taking their nap, she invited me to sit with her in the garden or in the lovely sunroom if she was not busy. As we enjoyed our afternoon tea, she told me about her life in England before the war and how the war had changed her country. She tearfully confided that she hoped one day her family might be able to go back to England, that she missed her mother and other relatives very much.

Our conversations made me aware she was a very lonely and unhappy person. She confided that my coming into her life had given her a joy she had not felt in many years because she did not feel isolated anymore.

Mrs. Pease always inquired about my husband and said she looked forward to meeting him. It was several more weeks before Ernie was able to come home for the weekend. The Pease family took a liking to him instantly, especially the boys. Ernie played with them, showing them how to do somersaults on the grass and impressing them with his gymnastic skills. When the time came for him to leave, they clung to him and begged him not to go. Evidently, no male adult had ever taken time to play with them before. He became Uncle Ernie to them, and they looked forward to his visits.

Mother had never been comfortable discussing sex with me, and assumed my husband would teach me what I needed to know. One day, much to my surprise, I discovered I was pregnant. I was not prepared for this and had no clue as to what I should do. I worked up the courage to tell Mrs. Pease. She was surprised when I told her and tried to hide her disappointment, but after a while, she wished me well and hoped that I would stay even after the baby came. She reminded me how much the boys depended on me and how attached they had become. I told her I liked living with them very much, that actually, it was the happiest home I had ever known, and I had no intentions of leaving. The decision, however, would depend on what Ernie wanted us to do.

Six months into my pregnancy, I began having severe pains in my lower back and abdomen that lasted all day. By nighttime, the pains were so severe I had to be taken to the hospital. I was rushed into the delivery room because I had been in labor all that time and did not know it. The next morning, the baby was born dead. It had died in my womb.

Mrs. Pease felt terrible and was concerned that she might have overworked me, and perhaps that had caused the premature death. I tried to assure her that I did not think so. Even the doctor was at a loss and could not determine what had caused the baby to die. My heart ached. I was very upset at the loss of my baby boy. I was not allowed to see him, and for many years, I cried whenever I thought of him. After one week in the hospital, I was discharged. Mrs. Pease paid the bill and took me to her house to recuperate.

Ernie came home two weeks later, full of apologies and saying how sorry he was that he had not been able to come home during my hospital stay. He told me his discharge papers were in process, and with such short notice, he was not permitted to leave. Now that he was home to stay, he announced one night that he had given our future plans a lot of thought. He convinced me we should move to Cleveland and stay with his folks for a while to give him time to decide what he should do next.

After being with the Pease family for ten months, I had to leave. I felt like I was being torn apart because I wanted to stay with this family, yet I wanted to be with my husband. I stayed three more weeks to give Mrs. Pease time to find my replacement and for me to train the new nanny. Poor

Mrs. Pease went around dabbing her eyes, equally torn over my leaving. The household took on an air of mourning while I packed my belongings.

Saying goodbye to my mother was going to be even more difficult. I realized this would be the first time in my young life that we would live so far apart. I really hated to face that day.

8

BETRAYAL

When we arrived in Cleveland, I was happy to find that my in-laws were the kindest and most loving people I could have asked for. It was evident from the onset that they favored their son Ernie, and before the first day ended, they treated me as another daughter. Mrs. Cafege was the epitome of a caring mother, so lovable you just wanted to hug her. With her permission, I immediately began calling her Mom. Being from Greece, she mainly spoke Greek, so her English was limited. However, I had no trouble understanding her as she took me under her wings. I delighted in learning to cook many wonderful Greek dishes. Her specialties were stuffed grape leaves, egg and lemon soup, roast lamb, fresh salad with feta cheese and olive oil, and several delicious desserts such as baklava. My father-in-law was a caring person with a big heart who was quick to tears. He was small in stature, with a large nose and a ruddy complexion. He had established his own shoeshine business in one of the hotels downtown, and like all the men of his generation, he retained his old customs. After the evening meal, he would go to the coffeehouse down the street to join his friends. As a result, he was seldom home.

After living with them for nearly two months, we finally found a fully furnished one-bedroom apartment. Within a week after getting settled, Ernie found a job in the mailroom with the local newspaper, and I was hired by a high-fashion house that specialized in making suits and coats for men and women. On Sunday, the entire family gathered for lunch at our in-laws, a family tradition that had been established long ago in Greece.

My life was interrupted once again when Ernie decided to enroll in college to study journalism. He had applied at the University in Albuquerque, New Mexico, and was accepted. After being in Cleveland for only eight months, we had to prepare to move again. It was disturbing having to leave his family because we had formed a close and loving relationship. My hope was that this move would be a lasting one.

Before leaving Cleveland, Ernie had somehow managed to save enough money to buy a car, a Pontiac Bonneville. This was an unexpected surprise and made the long trip comfortable and more exciting. As we traveled across the western states in style, the western plains and mesas captivated me. My eyes became a camera, capturing the unusual changing views.

New Mexico was different from any place I had ever seen before. I saw American Indians for the first time and marveled at the Navajo women wearing their colorful blankets around their shoulders, enhanced by the fabulous silver necklaces called squash blossoms around their necks. When we entered Albuquerque, my mind raced with excitement at the anticipation of my new life and a home.

Before we left Cleveland, Ernie had visited the University of New Mexico by himself. He took a week off from work and drove to Albuquerque to check out the campus. After he registered, he stayed several more days to look for a place for us to live. Now, as we approached the center of town, he pulled up in front of a modest house and parked the car. He turned off the engine and took my hands into his, and while looking intently into my eyes, began telling me there was a problem he had not wanted to tell me about until now. He explained that when he went to Albuquerque by himself, he had not actually found an apartment, but while looking at the ads in the newspaper, one caught his attention. The advertisement was for a couple to share a private home with a room for rent. He met with the owners and accepted their conditions. While parked in front of the house he pointed to it and announced, "This is going to be our home for now!"

That sounded reasonable to me, but Ernie had not told me the whole story. The agreement they had made was that, in exchange for the rent, I would have to take care of the wife. Mrs. Williams was an invalid in a wheelchair. She was paralyzed from the neck down, unable to walk or do anything. My other duties would include cleaning the house, doing the laundry, and cooking all the meals for the four of us. Our rent was for a one furnished bedroom, with a private bathroom in the hall, and we would share the living room.

When Ernie told me this, I froze in disbelief and felt betrayed. My heart began pounding in my chest and I thought I would faint. Seeing I was so upset, Ernie showed his annoyance by raising his voice and shouting at me for the first time, "Like it or not, this is going to have to do!"

He had never raised his voice to me before, and it sent shock waves through my body. The tightness that filled my throat began to choke me, but I held back my tears. My reaction made him relent somewhat, and he promised that if the arrangement did not work out, we would look for another place and move.

Had the woman been pleasant, it might have worked out, but she turned out to be the most bitter, mean-tempered, miserable person I had ever met. She complained about everything I did. I could not please her, no matter how much I tried. Her attitude and behavior toward her husband was deplorable. I have no idea how he tolerated her.

As the weeks went by, I understood why he stayed away much of the time. I now became the target of her anger and frustrations and had to bear her constant yelling. "Get me this. Get me that. Do this. Do that. No, do not do it that way. I want it now!"

Pleasing Mrs. Williams was impossible, and her unabated complaints made me a nervous wreck. The first month that we lived with them, I spent most of my nights crying myself to sleep. Since she was confined to a wheelchair, I had to help her with all her needs. I helped her in and out of bed. If she needed to use the toilet, I had to help her out of her wheelchair and onto the toilet seat, wipe her front and backside, and even change her sanitary napkins. I had to bathe and dress her every day and feed her like a baby. Her husband refused to feed her because she was verbally abusive to him all the time. Their constant verbal abuse would end up in heated arguments.

Keeping up with the laundry was another matter. It took the better part of an entire day. The constant workload and the incessant demands for my attention left me without a minute for myself. I did feel sorry for Mrs. Williams, knowing what a sad life she lived, and I tried to cheer her up by reading to her every day. Nothing made her smile, though, and nothing changed her attitude. She was bitter and seemed to find comfort in her misery by being difficult and mean to everyone.

This sad state of affairs was worsened by the fact that Ernie and I had no privacy. We had to stay in our bedroom most of the time and talk in whispers because we knew they listened to our conversations. In order to have some privacy, we would go for a ride after dinner. This situation was far from the home I had envisioned when we left Cleveland.

I tolerated this living hell for three months. Then one day, I reached a breaking point. When Ernie came home for lunch, I burst into tears and told him, "I have to get out of here as soon as possible, before I lose my temper, or worse still, my sanity. I cannot live in this house under these circumstances another minute. I feel as if I'm choking most of the time, having to hold back my pent-up emotions."

He agreed that the situation was intolerable and promised to start looking for another place right away. It took a month before Ernie found us a furnished one-bedroom unit that was available in an apartment building. Being a college town, it was probably the only thing that would be available for a long time, so we moved. In spite of the meager accommodations, we could not wait to get out of the Williams's house fast enough. Within two days, we were settled into our one-room home.

The building was a seven-story tenement, and our room was on the third floor. We were told that we would have to share the bathroom at the opposite end of the hall with the other tenants on our floor. The bedroom was about ten feet square, with barely enough space to walk between the bed and the four-drawer dresser. The only other piece of furniture was a single straight chair. To our dismay, the closet was not much wider than the door.

Thank goodness, we were allowed to cook in our room. We wasted no time in buying a two-burner hot plate, which we kept on top of the dresser. We later purchased a frying pan and a small pot. It amazed me how much we were able to cook in our makeshift kitchen. We also had a percolator coffee pot to brew our morning coffee on the hotplate. I knew this was temporary, and being young and carefree, it was actually fun, like camping out. Anything was better than what we had put up with for the past months. Now at least we had total privacy, a luxury in my estimation.

During the day, Ernie attended classes at the university, and in the evening, he worked in the mailroom for the local newspaper company. Finding myself with a lot of free time, I became bored and decided it was time to start looking for a job. Within a few days, I was hired as a salesclerk in Hinkel's Department Store, the largest store in town. Not only was it an ideal job, but also it was only two blocks from our apartment and within walking distance. I started working in the ladies' sportswear department. Within four months, I was transferred to better dresses and suits. Some time later, I was asked to be a model for both departments. This not only was a dream come true, but the modeling helped in getting over my shyness.

The management had a policy of training all the salesclerks in as many departments as possible. That way, if someone was out sick or if the department was short during a special sale, we would all be familiar with the merchandise. In another few months, I was transferred to the jewelry department. That was considered a promotion and meant that I had proven myself trustworthy, dependable, and well groomed. Appearances were very important. The department sold only top-quality gold jewelry, diamonds, and some high-quality costume jewelry. When a new shipment arrived, I would be the first to unpack the boxes and could admire the necklaces, pins, rings, and pearls. Of course, I couldn't afford to buy any of them, but it was great fun to dream that one day I might own jewelry as fine as what we sold.

I slowly began adjusting to my new life, but it was not very exciting. Actually, it was boring because during the day, Ernie was in school, and at night, he was at work. We hardly saw each other. One night Ernie came home and announced that he had sold our car and had traded it in for a Harley-Davidson motorcycle. He told me he sold it because it was necessary to cut down on our expenses. It took a while for me to get over my shock and disappointment, but when I learned to relax, I did enjoy riding on the back during our weekend outings. We started visiting places like Santa Fe and the Sandia Mountains outside of town whenever possible. Sometimes we would even stop for lunch at a Mexican restaurant if our budget allowed it, a special treat for me. At last, I was having fun again.

Feeling unusually sad and lonely, I decided to surprise Ernie at work one night. I had never been to his workplace before, so I took my time walking the five blocks it took to get to the newspaper building. When I arrived, I was tired and leaned against the corner of the building to rest for a minute. I knew it was about the time Ernie would be on his break, and I hoped we might be able to go for a cup of coffee and spend a few minutes together. I was about to enter the building when I heard the familiar sound of his motorcycle. The sound came from my right, so I looked in that direction to see if it was him. Excitement built up in me, knowing he would be surprised and happy to see me. It was his motorcycle, all right, and it was Ernie, but I'm the one who was surprised.

He pulled up to the curb about half a block from the newspaper building, and I saw a girl get off the bike from behind him. She leaned over and kissed him on the mouth as he held the back of her head close to him. My mouth went dry, as if it had been stuffed with a wad of cotton. My knees went limp, and I almost fell as I began to shake like a leaf. I quickly ran back around the corner of the building to hide, not wanting him to see me. Peering around the corner, I saw him grab her fanny and tussle her hair. They both were laughing like old lovers. After they stopped talking, she walked away, waving and throwing kisses at him. When she was out of sight, Ernie rode his bike toward the building, parked it in front, and went inside.

It took me several minutes to gain my composure. Actually, I had to work hard just to breathe. In a daze, I began to walk, then run, home. I had to stop several times to catch my breath and was blinded by my free-flowing tears.

How long had this been going on? I wondered.

When I arrived home, I threw myself across the bed and gave in to my emotions. I cried until there were no more tears left. I slowly began to see the situation as it really was, and the anger built up inside of me. My mind was racing, and I wondered how long they had been seeing each other. It was evident by the way they acted together that they knew each other intimately. I was dumbfounded and could not understand why he would do this to me. I had believed we were very much in love.

When I heard Ernie come into the room, it was close to three in the morning. I pretended to be asleep because I did not want to face the problem. Emotionally, I was not prepared to deal with it. The next night, I returned to his workplace at about the same time. I hid around the corner and again heard the familiar sound of his motorcycle. I looked around the corner and I saw the same girl get off his bike. The long kiss that followed was the same as the night before. I was devastated. Earlier, I had tried to convince myself that perhaps she was just a friend he had given a ride to. In my heart, I now knew this was not a chance encounter. The seriousness of what I had witnessed took time to register. I tried to convince myself that it was my imagination, but in the end, I had to face reality. The truth hurt so much that it was unbearable. For several days, I could not eat, nor could I think straight. What in the world was I to do? My mind was in turmoil. I felt helpless and alone.

As I pondered my situation, I came to the realization that there was not a single person I could confide in or ask for advice because I did not have even one close friend.

I threw myself on the bed, wanting to shut out the agonizing events I had witnessed. Then I was reminded of the comfort and advice I had received from my spiritual guardian in years past. After I married, I had stopped my nightly meditations, feeling secure in my husband's arms. I now willed myself to seek that meditative state, and in the stillness that followed, I was inspired to call my mother. I dreaded having to tell her because having to admit I had been deceived was humiliating. Knowing she was the only person I could turn to, I called her from a payphone the next day, crying uncontrollably and told her of my situation.

"Come home as soon as you can," she replied. "Give him a chance to explain himself, and tell him you're leaving. Emphasize that only if he changes his ways will you go back to him."

For several days, I mulled her reply over and over, building up the courage to do as she suggested. A few nights later, I went to Ernie's workplace one more time. I still did not want to accept the fact that he was cheating on me. Well, the same thing happened—same girl, same everything. I was now convinced. Like someone had hit me over the head with a two by four, the blow could not have been worse. When Ernie came home that night, I was sitting up in bed waiting for him, prepared for whatever the outcome would be.

"Who is the girl that you've been seeing?" I demanded.

"What are you talking about? You must be imagining things because you're alone so much. It's starting to affect your mind," he sarcastically replied.

Wow! I don't think it would have hurt any more if he had slapped me. I bolted off the bed and looked menacingly into his eyes while I pointed my finger barely an inch from his nose as I vented my anger. I told him exactly what I had seen. He was shocked and nearly speechless when he heard what I had done. His arrogance and indifference made me see that he really didn't care.

After regaining his self-assurance, he came back at me with a barrage of lies that made me wish I could choke him or claw his eyes out, just to shut him up. I did not want to even look at him anymore; he disgusted me so much. I now found the courage to tell him I was going to leave him because I no longer trusted him. With an air of defiance, his only response was, "That's fine with me."

A few days later, I packed my belongings and went back to New Hampshire.

* * *

When the war ended, Mother returned to New Hampshire because many factories no longer needed women workers and had to close. She had been one of the last women workers to lose her job. Arthur, on the other hand, stayed in Connecticut because he had been secretly dating another woman. When Mother found out, she ended their relationship. Instead of being sad, Mother was content to return to her roots and be close to her mother once again.

Luck was on her side when she located an apartment with three bedrooms, a rarity at the time. Terry and my brother Emile still lived with her, so when I arrived, it made for a very happy homecoming. At this point, we had not seen each other in almost two years, and the change in all of us was quite dramatic, especially Emile, who was now six feet tall and very handsome, with blonde curls and those beautiful brown eyes. He was eighteen and dating a girl I had known in the convent. As a matter of fact, she was a girl whose arm I had accidentally broken while playing tag in the convent yard one morning. My punishment had been to take care of her needs until she recovered. We had been good friends as young girls, but when she left the convent much sooner than I had, we lost touch with each other. It was going to be wonderful to see her again.

Terry at this time was dating a man older than she was by nearly twenty years. I told her I felt she was making a big mistake, but her mind was made up because she was madly in love with him. Even Mother was against the courtship, but Terry would not listen to any advice. She ended up marrying Eddie two months later.

By now, Mother had returned to work at one of the textile mills. The mills were no longer the sweatshops they had been before the war, and the pay scale had improved considerably. World War II had boosted everyone's financial status, to the point that nearly everyone could now afford to own a telephone. Mother wanted to keep up with the times and had one installed. I was impressed, thinking she must be making a lot of money to be able to afford a telephone. I had forgotten that Terry and Emile were obligated to give her part of their salaries each week.

Within a few weeks after I had settled in with them, Ernie began calling, insisting we had to talk. He was relentless in begging me to come back. He swore he had learned his lesson and vowed that he would never cheat on me again. But I had other plans. My old friend Irene was recently divorced and was moving to Miami, Florida, and had asked me to go with her. We both wanted to have a fresh start and felt a need to be more independent.

Irene's offer was tempting, and I discussed the idea with my mother. She agreed that it was a good idea and said it would be a great experience for me. She believed it would scare Ernie and make him want to change his ways. I personally wanted to teach him a good lesson. I was not ready to go back under the circumstances, and definitely not on his terms.

Nearly two weeks later, the plans were finalized. Irene and I were on a Greyhound bus traveling the length of the east coast on our way to Miami, Florida. It took three or four days by motor coach to get there, and by the time we arrived, we were totally exhausted. Nonetheless, we were exhilarated at the prospect of living in a tropical paradise with the sun shining every day. We walked for several blocks from the bus station looking for a motel. After quite a few blocks, a sign in a restaurant window caught our attention. In bold letters it said, waitress wanted, apply within.

Irene and I looked at each other and, being hungry and tired, went inside and ordered the lunch special. The three-course meal cost one dollar.

After having sampled the delicious food, we asked to speak to the owner. After a short introduction, Mr. C. sat at our table. We let him know we had just arrived in town and wanted to apply for the waitress jobs. After a short interview, he hired us on the spot and said to come to work the next day. We told him we had to find a place to live first, and since we had just arrived in town, we did not know where to look. He picked up the phone and called a friend who owned an apartment building about four blocks from the restaurant. After hearing our story, the owner told Mr. C. for us to come over right away to look at the only apartment he had available. The efficiency apartment suited our needs perfectly, and we paid the first week's rent. Our problem was resolved so effortlessly that I wondered if my guardian was instrumental in helping us. It felt magical. At the time, I did not know about divine intervention.

When we reported for work the next day, we learned our meals were included, along with our pay. After that, we made sure we arrived early every morning to enjoy a good breakfast before the long day ahead. By the end of the first week, I saw that the restaurant was very popular and in a prime location. The place was always full.

As a result, the tips bulged in our pockets at the end of each day. By the end of the week, Irene and I had more than enough money to pay for our next week's rent. Receiving tips was a great way to have constant ready cash. For the first time in my adult life, I was independent and learning to survive on my own. I was free and loving every minute.

Mother was right; I needed this experience. We called each other several times a week, and when the first month ended, she began suggesting that maybe I should give Ernie another chance. He called her constantly, demanding she tell him where I was. His repeated phone calls put pressure on her, and his promises of never treating me that way again weakened her resolve. She now began telling me I should give him another chance. The seed had been planted.

Her urging made me think about my vows. I was married for better or for worse. When I thought about Ernie, my long separation made me remember only the good times, and I now focused mainly on the fun we used to have.

Irene kept saying it was a mistake to go back and repeatedly said people don't change. "You'll be sorry if you take him back," she warned.

She reiterated that she had gone through a similar situation with her husband, and after several tries at reconciliation, she finally had to accept the truth: he was never going to change.

Eventually, my belief that Ernie loved me enough to change won out. Irene begged me to think it over carefully and to reconsider. I told her my mind was made up, that I planned to leave in two weeks. The owner and the employees gave me a going-away party, but Irene refused to attend. I'm sorry to say that my leaving ruined our friendship. Even though I tried to get in touch with her many times, she refused to have any further contact with me.

After having been gone for six months, I was on a Greyhound bus heading for New Hampshire. My thoughts were of Irene. As I traveled, a strong sense of foreboding began making me uncomfortable. At this time, I had not yet formed the habit of listening to my inner voice or my intuition. As we approached the bus terminal, I could see that Ernie was waiting for me, and at the sight of him, my stomach fluttered, and I ran into his arms. Two days later, after a short visit with my family. We left for Albuquerque, New Mexico.

While I was away, Ernie had moved out of the one bedroom we had lived in and had bought a second-hand house trailer. It was in excellent condition and consisted of one bedroom, a sitting area with a table, and a fully furnished kitchen. I was amazed to see that so many necessities could be arranged in such a small space. Ernie had parked it next to the house of his new friends, Joe and Dorothy, a couple he had befriended while I was away. They were older than Ernie, which made them much older than me, and I preferred to stay away from them as much as possible.

Unfortunately, our trailer was hooked up to their house for water and electricity, plus we had to use the bathroom located inside their house. I cringed whenever I had to go inside their house because it was always dirty and cluttered. They owned several acres of land, and the outside looked like a dumping ground, with old rusty cars, rusty machinery, and trash of every description scattered everywhere.

Our little trailer was cramped but certainly better than the one room we had lived in before. Within the first week, I got my old job back at Hinkel's Department Store, again in the jewelry department. My former coworkers welcomed me back with open arms, and even my boss kept saying how much everyone had missed me.

After four months of this joyful interlude, I began to notice that Ernie was coming home late many nights. When I questioned him about it, he always had a ready excuse. Wanting to believe he was telling me the truth, I ignored the gnawing feelings in the pit of my stomach. I knew if I questioned him any further, it would only start trouble, so I chose to dismiss the nagging thoughts that were invading my mind.

Soon afterwards, I discovered I was pregnant. I was truly happy and could not wait to tell Ernie. When he came home that night, I excitedly told him, but his weak response was not what I had expected. "Oh really, that's nice."

My joy turned to apprehension. Some time later, I noticed that a few of my wedding gifts were missing. I asked Ernie about them over dinner one night, and he made some lame excuse. I could tell by his eyes that he was lying. That familiar gnawing persisted, making me aware that I must be on my guard. My inner voice kept warning me that something was not right. I wrote Mother to tell her of my pregnancy but did not mention the problem I was having with Ernie. I hated to admit that I might have made a terrible mistake in coming back. It was too late for regrets, since I was now several months pregnant.

I was elated to be expecting a baby to replace the one I had lost. Not a day had gone by that I did not think of my little boy. I often wondered what he would have looked like. I remembered the pain of the labor and the anguish of my loss only too well, but the overwhelming desire to hold this new life in my arms made all the risks disappear and my happiness overpowering.

Mother wrote to say she was overjoyed to hear the news and that she would come to Albuquerque the week before the baby was due, to be with me when the baby arrived. Knowing my mother would be with me made my life more tolerable.

We had lived in the trailer for nearly six months when we began looking for a house to purchase. The need for a bathroom that I could use in a hurry prompted the urgency. The morning sickness had lasted three months and had been awful. In my sixth month, I was still having problems, and they led to my having to quit my job. I hated to leave, since that was my only contact with other people.

Within a few weeks, we found the perfect house. It was being built by an independent builder and nearing completion. Ernie applied for a V.A. loan, and within a month, the loan was approved. He sold the trailer to the builder in exchange for lowering the price of the house. With the extra money, we were able to buy all the furniture we needed. Shortly after the house was finished, we moved in. At last, we had two bedrooms, a large living room, a very big kitchen with a dining area, and finally, a bathroom with a bathtub. You cannot imagine what a luxury this represented to me.

In 1947 women were forming canasta clubs in nearly all the neighborhoods. My next-door neighbor Patty came to visit me one day and invited me to join their group. She told me they met one day per week and they needed one more person to complete the group. I was thrilled to be asked, since this would give me the chance to meet some of the other women in our neighborhood. I gladly accepted her kind invitation.

I looked forward to the canasta games. We would break for refreshments and go at it again until late afternoon. It was wonderful having new friends, but better still, one day a week I was not alone. For some reason, Ernie did not like the idea of my getting chummy with our neighbors. He wanted me to stay home and was extremely domineering. I had to account for every minute of my day. He was still going to school during the day and working for the same newspaper company at night. This meant he was gone nearly all day and every night. We seldom saw each other except on weekends. Nothing had changed.

Ernie insisted on keeping the motorcycle, even though it was our only means of transportation. My advanced pregnancy meant I could no longer travel with him.

I spent my time listening to the radio or reading. Ernie kept me supplied with books from the library and brought me a new supply every week. Reading kept me from being bored; each book transported me to another time or place where I would actually get lost for a while. The variety of subjects I read about provided a great way for me to educate myself, but being alone most of the time, I was lonely.

A friend came by one day and offered us a puppy from their new litter. She knew how much time I spent by myself and felt the puppy would be a good companion for me. He was part German shepherd and part Alaskan husky. He was so adorable that I fell in love with him right away. He had beautiful blue eyes and a coat of white and gray fur. We named him Rivet. He became my little buddy. At last, there was someone else in the house I could talk to and hug once in awhile. Since we lived on the outskirts of town, he was the perfect watchdog and great protection for me at night. I now understood why people became so attached to their pets. Rivet was my salvation.

A month later Patty came to see me. I was surprised, since she never came to my house. "I have to talk to you privately," she whispered. "Are you alone?"

I could tell this was not going to be a pleasant conversation. She began by telling me she had upsetting news that I should know about. She confided that whenever I left the house, Ernie would return a short time later with a girl on the back of his motorcycle.

"From my house, I can't tell if it's the same girl each time or a different one. I thought you would want to know. I'm so sorry to be the one to tell you."

With a lump in my throat, I thanked her. I was absolutely crushed. I knew there was no point in confronting Ernie. He would only deny it or make up some far-fetched story because he had become a master at telling lies. I felt like a puppet, and he was the master pulling the strings. I was angry at myself for being so gullible and weak. Although I suspected something was going on, I did not want to face it. Now I was forced to. I decided the best way to handle the situation was to catch him in the act.

A few days later, I told Ernie I wanted to go in town the next day to buy some items for the baby. When he left for school the next morning, I went to Patty's house. On my way, I thought it was strange how he had readily agreed to my leaving. That was so unlike him.

When I arrived at Patty's, she greeted me with a sisterly hug. Then we stationed ourselves by her living room window, where we had a perfect view of the front door of my house. We waited for forty-five minutes before we heard the familiar sound of Ernie's motorcycle. Sure enough, there was a girl sitting behind him on his bike. They ran into the house with their arms around each other. An hour and a half later, they emerged, quickly climbed on the bike, and left.

"You see, that happens all the time, shortly after you leave the house," Patty said.

I waited until I saw them far down the street, and when they turned the corner, I said goodbye to Patty and went back home. I was fearful of what I would find.

Rivet was chained to his doghouse outside and was barking incessantly. I hugged him and let my uncontrolled tears fall on his fur. After unchaining him, I brought him in the house to diminish my grief. When I entered my bedroom, I saw that my picture on the dresser had been turned face down and our bedspread was messed up, with his wet semen still noticeable on it. I sat on the floor and began sobbing.

Why is he doing this to me again? I wondered.

It was too painful to think about, and my body began shaking uncontrollably. I could not even stand up. I stretched out on the floor. My mind felt numb as I lay there in a state of disbelief. After a while, my body became weightless. It was as if I could not feel myself in the room. I was looking at myself from afar, observing the scene before my eyes. The room took on that familiar golden glow, like bright sunlight, almost blinding. I knew my spirit guardian had come to me, sensing my immense grief. For the first time I prayed, asking for protection and the strength to overcome the difficult days that lay ahead. Very clearly, I heard the words that gave me the strength I needed, "Don't worry. You will be protected. It's going to be all right."

The composure that came over me was instantaneous. I became so relaxed that I fell asleep on the floor. I was awakened when I heard Ernie close the front door. It was two o'clock in the morning. As he entered the bedroom, he exclaimed, "What in the world are you doing on the floor, especially in your condition?"

He actually looked concerned for a minute. I knew his game now, and I wasn't about to let him sweet-talk me into his web of deceit once again. Standing up, I told him exactly what I had done and what I had seen with my own eyes. He actually started to deny it. Can you believe it? I pointed out the spot on the bed, which had dried stiff by now, and pointed to my picture, which was still face down on the dresser. I was seething inside and was finally able to vent the anger I felt. Ernie was shocked to learn that I had tricked him; he never expected me to react this way. His anger flared up, reaching a pitch as strong as mine.

To get his revenge and get back at me, he began telling me of the countless affairs he had while I was away. The smirk on his face as he told me of his sordid affairs showed how much he reveled in the hurt he was inflicting on me. I learned in detail about his involvement with a waitress from the restaurant we used to go to frequently and with a woman who ran the Laundromat in our neighborhood.

He also wanted me to know that the girl he had brought home on the motorcycle was the same one he had had an affair with when I left him. He added that he was also seeing my friend, the one woman in our canasta group whom I believed was my best friend. Come to think of it, Ernie had been the one who had encouraged me to form a friendship with her.

That new revelation felt like someone had punched me hard in the stomach. Knowing there was no turning back, he inflicted the crowning blow. He wasn't finished with his mental abuse, and like a dam had broken, he let it all out of his demented soul.

He sarcastically informed me that while I was in Miami, he had gotten a girl pregnant and married her in order to give the baby a last name. Then he had arranged a quick divorce before I came back. He believed I would never find out, since I wasn't the type to ask questions. His denials and lies had been a constant torment, but these new revelations were more than I could handle. I blocked my ears with my hands and ran out of the room. He yelled, "The little convent girl is finally waking up, I see!" mocking my background.

He screamed for me to come back, but I ignored him. I locked myself in the bathroom and stayed there for the rest of the night. I thought about the spirit guardian who always came to help me during my difficult periods, but I wondered why I was not warned ahead of time. The answer I heard was, as humans, we are allowed to use our free will in order to learn to endure unpleasant circumstances. They are meant to teach us lessons that help us develop a strong character. The role of a guardian is to protect. It is up to us to communicate with them when we need guidance and help.

When I emerged from the bathroom, the revulsion and disgust I felt for Ernie helped release me from his control. I knew he could not hurt me anymore because that night I learned that I was to listen to my intuition; it is the spiritual voice we are born with that warns and guides us. I vowed I would listen carefully and never again allow anyone to control me.

9

MOTHERHOOD

My life during this period was the most difficult I have ever endured. I was sad most of the time, and having to live with Ernie was difficult. Whenever he came near me, I cringed, wanting to avoid him as much as possible. In my ninth month of pregnancy, Mother arrived one week before my due date. Having her with me cheered me up, and my life became a bit more pleasant. We spent the time planning for the baby's arrival by making little outfits. Mother never tired of knitting and crocheting tiny sweaters and booties. I was able to laugh as we reminisced about the old days and the happy family gatherings.

Not wanting my mother to know what I was going through, I tried to stay positive, but she was no fool and asked me one day what was bothering me. She commented that I did not seem to be my usual happy self. I was surprised because in my mind I thought I had carried on a convincing façade. I tried to convince her that everything was fine, but like most mothers, she knew I was not being honest. Had she known about my problems, I feared she would have brought up the subject with Ernie, and that would have infuriated him. He no doubt would have told her to leave. I wanted to avoid that distinct possibility by being extremely cautious whenever I was with the two of them.

Within a week of Mother's arrival, I began sensing that something was wrong. The due date had passed and I was not having any labor pains. I began worrying that Mother's vacation would end before the baby came. I started to meditate and pray at night, asking God to be with me during the new ordeals I faced. It became clear to me that the help I received was coming from a divine source. Two days later, my water broke as I was preparing breakfast. Mother ran to Patty's house and asked her to drive us to the hospital.

I continued having labor pains after we arrived, but they were mild. After several hours of labor, Dr. Parker informed me that he would have to induce my labor further and injected something into my abdomen. The severe labor pains started immediately and lasted most of the day, making me scream with every excruciating contraction. Around four in the afternoon, my baby girl Linda was born.

I was not allowed to see her until the next day, when she was brought to my room for a feeding. She was very tiny and frail looking, but she had the cutest round cheeks. I tried to breast feed her, but she kept falling asleep. I tried tickling her under her feet to keep her awake, but nothing worked. After half an hour of trying to keep her awake, her head went back and fell limp across my arm. I screamed for a nurse, thinking my baby had died since she was not responding.

The nurse quickly took the baby back to the nursery, and the next thing I remember was Dr. Parker at my bedside with a release form for me to sign. He said they had to give the baby a transfusion immediately because they discovered I was Rh-negative and my husband was Rh-positive. Our blood was incompatible. This was a newly discovered birth problem at the time. The baby had been born with too few red blood cells—not enough to sustain life. She was close to death and needed blood right away.

You cannot imagine the panic and fear that consumed me at that moment. The doctors searched the entire hospital staff for a donor. As luck would have it, one of the nurses on duty had the matching blood type. She was a young Mexican girl named Gloria. I thanked God that my prayers had been answered.

Several doctors were called in, forming a team to perform the rare and delicate first transfusion. The baby's veins collapsed during the first attempts, and they frantically tried to locate another vein somewhere. After quite some time, the surgeon decided to cut both of her inner arms inside the elbows and succeeded in finding a vein that would accept only a few cc's of blood. It was a small amount, just enough to keep the baby alive overnight.

On the second day, the team of doctors searched for a vein that would accept another transfusion, in order to keep the baby alive another night. After several attempts, they located a vein by cutting one of her ankles. Each procedure the doctors tried was performed without anesthesia because Linda was so tiny. Mother and I held each other and cried as we continually heard her scream. Ernie was nowhere to be found.

On the third day, they cut both her groin areas in order to locate a vein that would accept another 200 cc's of blood. Later that day, Dr. Parker came into my room after the surgery to tell me what they had done. He tried to conceal his tear-stained eyes as he began telling me in a quivering voice that the team had done everything they could. He stressed that the baby could not go through another operation and said she was now in God's hands. He held my hand as he whispered, "She will have to fight for her own survival. Her will to live will determine the outcome."

For five agonizing days, Mother and I, along with the nurses and some of the other patients, gathered in the hallway outside the operating room to pray on our knees asking God to please let her live. The nurse who had donated her blood came by every day to inquire about Linda, and she joined us in prayer whenever she could. I remember so well how we clung to each other while crying our eyes out and sharing our grief. After ten agonizing days, my baby began to rally and show signs of slow progress.

I was discharged from the hospital on the tenth day and was told that Linda would have to remain in intensive care for at least a month, perhaps longer depending on her progress. Being a twenty-year-old mother faced with going home from the hospital without my baby was an incredibly heart-breaking experience.

Mother had by now overextended her stay and would have to leave. She made the necessary arrangements to leave a few days later. Believe me, the day I took her to the bus stop, I was devastated. Watching the bus pull away and seeing her disappear from view was like having part of me torn away.

Going home to a loveless house was terrifying. I don't know how I would have survived that period of my life if I had not had the comfort of my spiritual guardian. In my dreams, I visited the divine source that would get me through the next day. I knew that this was my guardian angel or my spirit guide, who watched over me and gave me strength. I cannot explain the direct link or connection; it was just so natural to me. This unexplainable divine help is what guided me through the rough times that lay ahead. I instinctively knew my guardian was a messenger from God.

Three weeks had gone by since I had been discharged from the hospital, and my daily visit to the hospital by bus took up most of my mornings. I had just arrived home from the bus stop one day when a car pulled up in front of my house. It was late in the afternoon. Peeking through the window, I saw a well-dressed woman come to the front door. We seldom had visitors, so I wondered who this woman could be. I imagined she must be lost and wanted to ask directions. I opened the door, and smiling, said, "Yes, may I help you?"

She looked at me with a surprised look on her face and replied, "Is Ernie here? I have to talk to him."

"No, he's still at work," I replied.

Without hesitating, she blurted out, "Who are you? Are you a cleaning lady, or perhaps a relative?"

Taken aback, I said, "Of course not. I'm his wife!"

I thought the woman was going to faint. After the blood rushed back to her cheeks and she had regained her composure, she whispered, "May I come in? You and I need to have a talk."

I couldn't imagine what this woman, with her fancy car parked in front of my house, wanted to talk to me about. I could see that she was refined and wealthy, and I felt uncomfortable in her presence. My curiosity had peaked, however, so I invited her in. She looked me up and down several times with an inquisitive look on her face, then finally blurted out, "Okay, I may as well come straight to the point. Are you *sure* you are married to Ernie?"

"Of course, I am! What kind of ridiculous question is that?" I said.

I told her that Ernie and I were married in Cleveland, Ohio, right after the war ended, a little over two years earlier. To convince her, I had to show her our marriage license, which I kept in the cedar chest in my bedroom. The shocked expression on her face when she read it made me uncomfortable. It finally dawned on me that her purpose for being here was no doubt to deliver bad news. She began, "I don't know exactly how to tell you this because I'm sure it will upset you greatly. My daughter Leslie and Ernie have been dating for many months and are planning on getting married. In fact, the invitations have been mailed and the church wedding is set to take place next month. The engagement was announced in last week's newspaper. Ernie has been to our house many times and has met our entire family. He met my daughter at the university they both attend. By the way, I am one of the professors there. I teach American history."

I was taken aback to hear all this, but once your heart has been broken into a million pieces, I suppose it generates its own anesthesia. Her words did not hurt me, but they did shock me. The pain of Ernie's recent confession came rushing back. Now hearing about this new encounter with yet another girl merely added fuel to the already raging fire I felt within. I regained my composure and informed her this was not the first time Ernie had done this to me. He had been unfaithful to me our entire married life.

I informed her that I had just given birth to a baby girl three and a half weeks earlier and explained how she had nearly died at birth, adding that she was still in the hospital in intensive care. I felt the urge to unburden myself to her and told her about my years with Ernie and his unbelievable infidelities. As I talked, her eyes got bigger with each revelation. The man she had grown to love as a potential son-in-law was a fraud, a wife abuser, and a sadist. Her eyes became glassy with unspent tears as she empathized with me. As a caring mother, Mrs. Connor could not control her anguish any longer and came rushing toward me. She took me in her arms, and while embracing me, cried uncontrollably on my shoulder, repeating over and over again, "You poor unfortunate girl"

She could not believe how any man could do this to his wife. What could I say? I did not know the reason myself. The conversation ended, and a heavy silence engulfed the room.

It became apparent that she was in no hurry to leave, so I invited her to stay for coffee. Mrs. Connor then asked me about my plans for when the baby was allowed to come home. I told her I had none because I knew nothing about how to take care of a newborn and I was afraid. She then offered, indeed insisted, that I let her be the one to drive me to the hospital when the time came so I could bring the baby home in a comfortable car instead of on a bus. She was filled with compassion and wanted to help me in every way possible.

I'm certain she was trying to make amends for the grief her daughter had caused me. I assured her I did not hold her daughter responsible. After all, the girl did not know that Ernie was married. Given his charming manner with women, I knew she had fallen under his spell, just as all the others and I had.

As we talked, our friendship deepened, and she asked if I would allow her to come to the house every day to check on me after I brought the baby home. She pledged to continue to do so for as long as she was needed. She wanted to be the one to show me how to bathe the baby, how to fold and change diapers, and how to sterilize the milk bottles, as well as make the formula. Without my mother or a close friend, those were all the things I had worried about regarding the day I would bring the baby home. I knew this must be divine intervention. How else could this have come about? I thanked God and my guardian for watching over me and sending the help I desperately needed.

We were still talking when Ernie came home. You can imagine the shock on his face when he walked in and saw us drinking coffee together and talking like old friends. He tried to make his entrance seem casual as he walked by. Smiling he said, "Well, hello!"

Mrs. Connor could barely control her anger when he walked past her with such an air of superiority. She jumped out of her chair and walked up to him. Standing directly in front of his face, she asked in a menacing voice, "Is it true that you are married to this young lady?"

She was testing him, of course, to see what his response would be. He had no way of knowing how long she had been there, nor what we had talked about, but he responded with a firm, "Yes, it is."

Without hesitating, she slapped him hard across the face. She screamed, "You are an unbelievable wretch! You are never to speak to or contact my daughter ever again! Do I make myself clear?" The look in her eyes was frightening as she continued, "Do you realize how many lives you have ruined by your selfish actions?"

Not being able to control her anger any longer, she felt it best to leave and waved goodbye to me as she walked out. I looked over at Ernie and saw the evil grin on his face. He didn't feel any remorse and wasn't a bit sorry. I'm sure he was relieved to be off the hook, so he could have the freedom to pursue his next love affair.

Mrs. Connor was well down the street when Ernie turned his anger toward me and began his barrage of verbal abuse and threats. I felt such revulsion toward him I could barely control my own anger. I knew that talking to him would be futile. He would make up more lies and waste my time. I ran out of the room and locked myself in the bedroom. I sat on the bed and waited patiently until I heard the roar of his motorcycle. This time, it was a pleasurable sound. He was out of the house. I could breathe again, and I unclenched my hands. Feeling relaxed, I went to bed and fell into a deep sleep.

True to her word, Mrs. Connor came to get me the day I was told I could bring my baby home. She also came every day for over a month. She would arrive early every morning until she felt certain I was comfortable caring for the baby by myself. Ernie made certain he was out of the house before she arrived.

On Mrs. Connor's last visit she hugged me for the longest time and said, "I want to forget the past. We both must try to erase this tragic event from our minds. It will be difficult, I'm sure, but eventually the pain will lessen. We will not see each other after today, and I wish you the very best."

We had formed a close attachment during those weeks, and I'm certain she had been an unexpected Godsend to help me in my time of need. The memory of that woman lingered with me throughout the years. Whenever I see a newborn baby, I am reminded of her, and I whisper a silent thank you.

At six weeks, Linda weighed only six pounds. As small as she was, her beautiful blue eyes were unusually large. Her cheeks were now pink with the red blood flowing through her veins, and her head was covered with blonde fuzz. She had a smile on her face, even when she was sleeping. I thought that was most unusual, especially knowing all the trauma and pain she had gone through. When I looked at her, I felt she was very happy to be here with me. This adorable bundle of joy became my universe.

During the passing weeks, Ernie continued his regular routine as if nothing had happened. Ever since Mrs. Connor's visit, Ernie made it obvious he no longer cared about how I felt. Yet, like a cat chasing its prey, he watched my every move. He again made sure I did not leave the house without his permission and insisted on doing all the shopping by himself. He asserted himself by becoming an unbearable tyrant. He expected his demands to be obeyed instantly and treated me like a servant, not his wife.

I resolved that I was not going to take his abuse anymore. I had put up with his behavior for the sake of the baby, thinking that being a family was the most important thing in a marriage. Growing up in a Catholic home, I was led to believe it was the only way. Ernie took my passivity as a sign of weakness and used my kindness against me.

Once in awhile, he tried his charming ways to win me over, but when he saw that they no longer worked, he began using a new tactic. He insisted a woman was her husband's property, that no matter what a husband wanted or did to his wife, she must submit to his every command without question. No matter how much he tried to make me obey him, I insisted that I had a mind of my own. I was not going to be treated like his possession.

I knew I desperately needed help and began lying in bed at night, calling out to my guardian to please help me. I deliberately went into my meditative state every night. After several days, guiding thoughts began forming in my mind. A plan emerged; all I had to do was carry it out. The belief that the idea would work fortified me. The time had come to stand up for myself.

I chose a day when I knew Ernie was in a good mood to tell him that I had an idea I wanted to discuss with him. I cautiously began by saying I wanted to visit my mother for a short time. I said I needed to be with my family for a while, adding that I felt our time apart might help us rekindle our love for each other. I knew full well that he would never agree to let me go without some sort of incentive. We actually discussed my idea for a few days, and he agreed to think about it. A few days later, he came home in a very friendly mood and handed me two hundred dollars, cheerily saying, "Here honey, this is for your birthday. Go visit your mother with Linda for a few weeks, but promise to call me often, okay?"

I was dumbfounded. This sudden change of heart made me suspect that he must be involved with a new love interest and wanted me out of the way for a while. That was fine with me because my objective was to get away from him as soon as possible. I wanted to eventually secure my own freedom.

I still could not believe he had agreed to let me leave. I was overjoyed but remained cautious for fear he might change his mind. I was fully aware that any little thing could trigger an argument and result in being told I could not leave. That was another one of his pleasurable forms of mental abuse and a means of controlling me. As I packed our belongings, I hummed a soothing tune to keep my nerves intact. It took quite a while to decide what necessities to pack for Linda and me, being aware that I was never coming back.

The next day, filled with excitement and holding the sleeping bundle in my arms, I boarded a plane for Boston, the closest airport to my hometown. I had never flown before, and the thought of it made me nervous. As we began taxiing away from the airport, getting ready to take off, my stomach made a few leaps, and I clung to the arms of the chair in sheer fright. Once we were airborne, I began to relax and took my first deep breath. With a comforting sigh, I looked down at my three-month-old baby, fast asleep on my lap and thanked God for sending the wonderful guardian who helped in forming the plan that made my escape possible.

10

INDEPENDENCE

While we were airborne, nagging thoughts crossed my mind. I wondered what on earth I was going to do to support myself and my baby in the days ahead. My intuition came into play, assuring me that I was making the right decision because, for my own sanity, I had to be free from Ernie. That it was an urgent necessity. Trusting in my divine inspirations calmed me, and closing my eyes, I began to relax.

What seemed like a short time but was actually many hours later, the pilot's voice informed us that we were descending and should prepare for our landing, interrupting my reverie. Walking into the Boston Airport was a sobering experience. I had not seen that many people in one place before in my entire life. The noise was deafening, with all the people who were scurrying to catch a flight. In the confusion, I did not know where to go.

I must have looked pathetic, with panic written on my face because a policeman approached me and asked if I was all right. I began crying, and in-between sobs, told him I felt totally lost. I explained that this was my first time to fly and I had to go on to New Hampshire, but I had just been informed that no planes or buses were scheduled to go there. I was stranded and did not know what to do. I added that I had been traveling from New Mexico and was unable to feed my baby because I had run out of formula. Poor Linda was crying because it was time for her next feeding, and I had used the last bottle on the plane. His fatherly instincts came to the forefront, and he quickly summoned a matron from the ladies' room. She told him there was a drugstore close by that would have the formula I needed. He called a young attendant who was standing by and sent him to buy it for me. I gave him the money to cover the cost, along with a tip.

The kind matron helped me prepare the formula while Linda wailed. After she finished the bottle, I changed her diaper and she quickly fell asleep. At last, I was able to concentrate on my next problem. How was I going to get to New Hampshire? To my surprise, the friendly policeman brought a cab driver over. He had explained that I needed someone to drive me to New Hampshire, and the cab drive agreed to take me to my mother's doorstep for $25.

That was a lot of money back then, but knowing it was the only way I could get home, I accepted. As it turned out the $25 was well deserved, especially because the driver would have to drive all the way back to Boston. When we arrived at our destination two hours later, he carried my luggage up the three flights of stairs. I knocked on Mother's door several times and discovered no one was at home. The driver asked if he could leave because he had to drive all the way back to Boston, and I told him yes, that I would be fine.

When I left New Mexico, it had happened so quickly that I did not have the time to call my mother. She did not know I was coming and bringing the baby. I looked around the landing and saw there was no suitable place to hide a key. I began pounding on the door even louder. When nobody answered, I was convinced no one was home. I sat on the stairs to rest. Then it dawned on me that I was hungry. I had not eaten since breakfast, and here it was, late in the afternoon. I changed Linda's diaper and gave her the last of her bottle. While doing this, deep in thought, an idea popped into my head. There must be a bus stop close by. Instinctively, I picked up the baby and the diaper bag and left the luggage, knowing it would be safe.

I walked down the three flights of stairs and hurried outside. Sure enough, there was a bus stop across the street. A few minutes later, a bus appeared, going in the direction where my grandmother lived. In less than ten minutes, I was within a block of her house. Getting off the bus while carrying Linda and the diaper bag was nearly too much for me. I hardly had enough energy left to walk the last few steps. As I reached Grandmother's front porch, a jolt of energy tingled through my body. It was like an electrical surge that made my heart pound fast. It was beating so hard that I felt it would pop out of my chest.

After several rings, the door swung open, and there stood my grandmother. I laughed when I saw the visible shock on her face as she realized it was me holding her newest great granddaughter. It had been over two years since we had last seen each other. She quickly took Linda from my arms and showered her with kisses, exclaiming she was the cutest baby she had ever seen. I followed her into her bedroom, and she gently placed Linda on her bed, putting pillows and covers all around her so she wouldn't roll off.

After making certain Linda was safe, we went to the kitchen. Grandmother asked if I was hungry, and when I told her I had not eaten since breakfast, she was flabbergasted. She quickly made me a wonderful meal. With my energy restored, I filled her in on the events of the past two years. Her mouth fell open a few times when I told her about Ernie, and she agreed that I had done the right thing in leaving him.

Before leaving Mother's apartment, I had written a note saying I was going to find my way to Grandmother's house and asking her to call me when she arrived home. After reading my note, instead of calling, Mother took the next bus and surprised us both.

She was shocked to hear that I had left Ernie, but upon hearing of the circumstances that prompted my decision, she was heartbroken yet proud that I had the courage to protect myself and my child. After talking for several hours and enjoying another fabulous meal, Mother and I left with my sleeping baby.

When we walked into Mother's apartment, it was obvious that some changes would have to be made. My brother Emile was still living with her, and I would need his room. As I expected, Emile was so happy to see the baby and me that he quickly offered us his room.

The next morning, when Mother and Emile left for work, I was alone at last with Linda. I could feel the tension literally ease from my body, and could finally breathe freely once again.

The first month went by smoothly. I did call Ernie as I had promised, making light of the family activities, so he would not become jealous. But, by the second month, he began asking when I was coming home. I told him I was not ready and made all sorts of excuses. Eventually, I found the courage to tell him the truth: I was not coming back. Ever.

Reverting to his old ways, he began threatening me. He started by saying I belonged to him, we were a family, and he would decide what was good for me. The next time he called and began screaming at me to come back, I hung up. After repeated phone calls I would not answer, it dawned on him that I was not going to listen to him anymore. When he realized he had lost control over me, he tried using new tactics. He began crying and begging me to forgive him. He promised he would never cheat on me again, adding that I was the only woman he had ever loved, that all those other women meant nothing to him.

As my commonsense came into play, my heart slowly healed. One day it dawned on me that scar tissue had formed a protective shield around my heart because I no longer felt any kind of emotion toward him. He may as well have been talking to a brick wall. That's when I knew I was truly free.

The time had come for me to find a job. I applied for work at several department stores, and within a few days, one contacted me. The manager was pleased with my previous experience and told me to start the next day. I was hired as a salesclerk in the better jewelry department. I had been in New Hampshire six weeks and now had a job.

Now that I was working, taking care of Linda became a serious problem. I was lucky to find a teenager who would come to the house to babysit when I went to work, but it was obvious she did not have any experience with a baby. I needed someone older and more mature, an older woman who would have commonsense and would be reliable. My grandmother babysat for me a few times, but it presented problems since she was not always available. I needed a permanent arrangement, but where to look? To keep my job, I would have to find someone soon.

I was constantly thinking of ways to solve this problem when I decided to resume meditating at night to ask for guidance. Soon ideas began forming in my mind, and after receiving my first paycheck the following week, I placed an ad in the local newspaper. Several women called, and I interviewed them over the phone. I selected a lady who had two teenage daughters. Her husband had been killed during the war, and she received a small pension—barely enough to support them. She confided that she desperately needed the extra income. I arranged to visit them the coming weekend, wanting to see if the house was kept clean. I brought Linda along to see how she would respond to them.

I was pleased to see that the house was immaculate, and learned that Mrs. Goslin loved babies and was an excellent cook. Her teenage daughters, Doris, fourteen, and Lanette, nearly thirteen, fell in love with Linda immediately. Linda responded with smiles and cooing. Both girls wanted to hold her. They treated her with extreme tenderness, like a precious doll. I could see that Linda would have four mothers to spoil her. This was the perfect home environment I was looking for.

The circumstances were so perfect that Mrs. Goslin and I agreed on the arrangements right away. Linda would stay with them during the week, and I would be free to visit her every night after work. On Friday night, I would take her home for the weekend, and then bring her back Sunday evening. This agreement worked out well for all of us.

As we became better acquainted, Mrs. Goslin invited me to stay for dinner many nights, and during the week, I frequently brought dinner for all of us. I saw Linda every night after work and knew that she was being well cared for. This made it possible for me to see her growing process and even hear her say her first words. I was with them the day she took her first steps. Linda was a very happy baby and had a smile on her face nearly all the time. What was unusual is that she seldom cried. As a new mother, I did the best I could under the circumstances, but I regretted not having a husband who could share her love.

After working for two months, I had saved enough money to afford a one-bedroom rental in a converted old house. It was not an ideal situation because, once again, I had to share the only bathroom on my floor with three other tenants. My bedroom was sparsely furnished and had the tiniest closet imaginable. The inconvenience was worth it, though, in order to have my own place with privacy. But I soon found out that living alone for the first time in my life was not as wonderful as I had imagined; it was depressing and extremely lonely. I often regretted having left the comfortable home I had shared with my mother.

* * *

My sister Theresa lived on the outskirts of town in an old lakeside house that was more like a shack. Some weekends, in order to get away from my own lackluster life, I visited her, bringing Linda along so she could get to know her cousins. I always left feeling more depressed than when I had arrived because Theresa had married Eddie, who was even worse than my father had been. I tried telling her to leave him for her own safety, but she would walk away, saying she just couldn't. Unfortunately, after I left, she would tell him what I had said. Before long, I was no longer allowed to visit her.

The next five months flew by, and Ernie finally accepted the fact that I was filing for a divorce. One year later, the divorce was finalized. I was the first person in our entire family to get a divorce. Just like that, a piece of paper gave me my freedom. Much later, I found out that being a divorced woman with a child put me in a category that many people looked down on. It was as if a scarlet letter was emblazoned on my chest.

The divorce decree ordered Ernie to pay me child support of thirty dollars a month. That was not enough to pay for Linda's daily care, let alone her clothes and other necessities. For three months, he sent the thirty dollars, then the checks stopped coming. Six months later, Ernie sold our house in Albuquerque and sent me half of the proceeds, which amounted to one thousand dollars. That was more money than I had seen in my whole life! I was overjoyed and deposited the money into my first savings account.

While I was working in the jewelry department one day, the store manager sought me out and said they needed help in the men's department right away. They were having a huge promotion to introduce men's shirts in colors for the very first time, and they were short of help. Up until that day, men had worn only white shirts, so this was indeed a big deal.

A display of shirts had already been placed in a large bin near the front door, and I began arranging them in neat color-coded piles, along with a display of colorful ties that blended nicely with the shirts. While I was busy doing this, a man stopped by to examine them. I approached him with a smile, and said, "Aren't these terrific?"

I went on telling him that colored shirts for men was the latest fashion in menswear, adding that he would look great in each of the colors. I then showed him the new ties and how well they looked with the gorgeous shirts.

I recommended several shirts and ties to go with them, which brought a smile to his face. He turned to me and said, "Young lady, you are by far the best salesperson I have ever encountered. I'll take a shirt in each color and this tie that goes well with all of them."

After I rang up the sale, I handed him the bagged items. He hesitated, then surprised me by saying he owned the exclusive women's dress shop a few blocks down the street. He introduced himself as Mr. Burnstein and said he was looking for a new sales manager for his store. He invited me to come by his store to discuss the manager's position at my convenience.

Three days later, I walked the few short blocks to his store for the interview. When I walked in, I was delighted to see that the shop was a boutique that catered to ladies who wanted elegant, more exclusive clothes. When Mr. Burnstein saw me, he was thrilled and rushed to greet me. I was on my lunch break, so he wasted no time in telling me what he was looking for in a manager. He mentioned that he especially liked that I was well dressed because that would make a good impression on his customers. He said he already knew I was an excellent salesperson, the main quality he was looking for. He felt certain I would learn the necessary requirements to manage his store in a short time. One added requirement would be to decorate the front windows twice a month. I assured him it would be a welcomed challenge because I was born with an interest in art and decorating the window displays would allow me to test my creative ideas. After that exchange, we both sensed that this was a match made in heaven.

He brought up the salary, and I tried not to show my surprise when the figure he offered was double what I was making at my current job. I knew I was taking on a lot more responsibility and the added work would test my managerial skills. I was confident that I could do it, being young, full of ambition, and excited by the challenges the job presented. It would give me the opportunity to prove I was capable of handling it all.

Besides a manager, Mr. Burnstein employed one other sales girl, named Julia. Part of my job would be to train her, teach her how to improve her selling skills, and insist she arrive on time. He also employed a full-time bookkeeper named David who came before the store closed each evening. He would count the money in the register, tally the receipts, and lock up. I was glad I would not have those responsibilities. I agreed to start in two weeks, wanting to give my current employer adequate notice. We shook hands to consummate the agreement.

Mr. Burnstein could not believe how fast I learned. He told me he owned two other stores in Lowell, Massachusetts, his hometown. He said he would have to leave soon, since he had neglected them for over a month. After my three weeks of training, he left me in charge and went back to Massachusetts. Mr. Bernstein called me twice a week to see if I needed help, saying I was to call him anytime. The last week of each month, he would come to the store to make sure that everything was going smoothly. Much to his surprise, the second month's sales had increased steadily. He was overjoyed, and we attributed the increase in sales to the window displays. I would change them whenever new merchandise arrived.

David, the bookkeeper, was very shy. It had taken him nearly two weeks just to say hello to me, always with his head down, afraid to make eye contact. His greatest quality was punctuality. You could have set your watch at precisely six o'clock, when he walked in the door. When he felt more comfortable with me, he confided that he was single and lived with his ailing mother, who was confined to a wheelchair. I felt sorry for him because I knew he had no personal life. His mother controlled his every action. I was glad when he walked in every night at closing time. Not having to clear the register and add up all the sales made my job a lot simpler. David could not believe how much the sales had increased in such a short time. He would scratch his head and say, "Wow, another record week."

Selling came as natural to me as breathing. I didn't think I was doing anything out of the ordinary because it was so effortless.

I looked forward to closing each night so I could spend a few hours with Linda before her bedtime. I wanted so much to be a good mother and to be with her as much as possible. God only knows how much I missed her. This longing prompted me to start looking seriously for an apartment because a bedroom with a shared bathroom down a long hall was not a place to bring up a child.

It took several weeks of looking before I found the perfect place quite by accident. While running an errand for the store, I was walking on a side street not far from where I worked when I happened to see a sign in the window of an apartment building: apartment for rent, apply with manager on the first floor.

The building was only three stories and had recently been restored, and the new paint on the outside gave it a brand-new look. I walked in and asked to see the manager. After a brief introduction, she took me to the second floor and showed me the rooms that were available. One look at the spacious newly painted rooms, and I knew I had found my dream home. It was bigger than my entire house in Albuquerque. Without hesitating, I gave the manager a down payment and returned the next day with the first month's rent.

With a secure well-paying job, I was in a position to get whatever I wanted. This became like an adventure, learning to survive on my own with a child to support. It was frightening and lonely at times, but working a full-time job and visiting with Linda at night left me little time for other pleasures. I was content to stay in my lovely apartment and read for relaxation.

After a few months of domesticity, I became bored and decided to start dating occasionally. Linda was two years old, and I began feeling the need for male companionship. I knew that dating was not going to be the same as when I was young, and the first few dates I went on were a big disappointment. The men seemed nice at first, but after dinner or a movie, they wanted to get me in bed on the first date. Some were down right forceful. Several times, I had to fight my way out of a car. They assumed that since I was divorced I was desperate.

My job was stimulating and provided me with daily encounters with interesting people. Staying busy with my countless job requirements was fulfilling as well. One of the most time-consuming tasks was the weekly ordering of new merchandise and unpacking the boxes when they arrived. I was always looking for ways to increase our sales, and since I ran the store, I told Mr. Burnstein I envisioned expanding our line of products. He agreed to have me try it on a limited scale. As the weeks went by, we increased our line of women's wear to include coats, purses, and underwear. I knew we would need extra help soon because the business was expanding rapidly. When the sales continued to increase, we hired three more salesgirls. A short time later, I received a substantial raise.

* * *

One week later, a man came to the store and asked for Mr. Burnstein. I told him he was not in but that he was expected later in the day. He asked me to give Mr. Burnstein a message and left. As I watched him leave the store and cross the street, my stomach fluttered. I knew instinctively that we would meet again.

The next day, just before closing time, the phone rang. I had been expecting a business call from the market in New York all day, and I rushed to answer it. To my surprise, it was an unfamiliar male voice asking me out to dinner, the same man who had asked for Mr. Burnstein the day before. His name was Milton. I could feel the blood rushing to my face. Not wanting to sound overly anxious, I told him I always visited my daughter after work, that the trip by bus took nearly an hour and a half before I returned home. I said I would be glad to have dinner with him afterwards. I figured he might as well know up front that I had a child. With fair warning, it would give him an excuse to back out if he wanted to. Surprisingly, Milton said he would be happy to drive me to see my daughter. This way, we could spend time with her and then leave afterwards for dinner, saving us precious time. It was settled.

I arranged for him to come to my apartment, which gave me time to clean up and change into a more suitable dress.

We spent an hour visiting with Linda, enjoying her attempts at talking, taking turns playing with her, and getting all the hugs we could muster in that short time. I told Mrs. Goslin I would not be able to give Linda her bath that night, and of course, she understood. We left shortly afterwards and headed for the country club outside of town. Never having been inside a country club before, I had no idea what to expect. Some of the golfers were still coming in after their rounds, looking mighty sharp in their golfing outfits. Their wives or girl friends waited for them in the bar where Milton escorted me. We ordered a drink—my first ever.

We later ordered dinner and sat eating by candlelight with fresh flowers on the table. I felt like the luckiest girl in the world. I could not believe that such a wonderful experience was happening to me. It reminded me of Mrs. Pease and how she had loved going to her country club every day to be with her friends. I could see now why she enjoyed it so much. This luxury could become addictive.

We both knew the evening must end, and as we rode home in silence, Milton reached for my hand and kissed it, sending chills down my spine. When he unlocked the door to my apartment, he turned to me and said he would be away for at least ten days. He wanted to know if he could call me when he returned. With my heart pounding in my chest, I managed to say, "Of course you may."

As I watched him go down the stairs, I felt a yearning that was a new sensation for me.

Time has a way of standing still when you're looking forward to something, and the ten days seemed more like a month. Finally, the day arrived when Milton was due back. As I began covering the merchandise before closing the store, the shrill sound of the telephone made me jump. Milton's voice on the other end was comforting. He excitedly said, "Hi there, it's me. Are you closing soon? I can hardly wait to see you again."

I told him I was almost finished and would be out front in five minutes.

I had already alerted Mrs. Goslin that if I was not there by seven, it meant I would not be coming to visit Linda that night. As I approached the car, Milton held the door open for me and we sped off to the country club for another fabulous evening. We spent the rest of the night in his room, locked in each other's arms.

This established a new routine. Whenever Milton was in town, we spent several hours alone with Linda and then headed out to the country club. After a few weeks, he insisted that I shop for all of Linda's clothes in his children's store, adding he would pay for them. Once I felt comfortable doing so, she never lacked for anything. He also told me to buy my sister's three children whatever they needed, and those purchases became an incredible blessing. While he was away, Milton called often to say how much he loved me and that he could not stop thinking about me. After several months, he began adding, "All I want is for us to be together forever."

At last, I was very content and happy. Milton's words made me start to think about how nice it would be if he and I were married because it would make it possible for Linda to live with us full time. My mind fixated on that thought. When we had been seeing each other for nearly a year, I decided to bring up the subject. His first response was to say he would have to think about it.

A few weeks later, during dinner, he shattered my world by telling me he was married. He quickly added that he did not love his wife, and the only reason they stayed together was because of their two daughters. When he pulled out their pictures from his wallet to show me what they looked like, I felt revulsion towards him. My trust in Milton was shattered, and I felt totally used. I pulled my hand away from his, and tears welled in my eyes. I was barely able to control my emotions but had the courage to say, "I'm very sorry to hear this. I wish you had been honest with me from the beginning. I even told you several times I never wanted to be involved with a married man. You carried on this deceit in spite of that. Please, there is nothing more you can say. Take me home. I can't stand to be here with you another minute."

As he unlocked my door, he held me around the waist. I allowed him to kiss me one last time. We held each other for a long time, sobbing uncontrollably. After pulling away from him I said, "Goodnight, and goodbye, Milton. I will never forget you. But please, do not call me anymore, because I will no longer accept your calls."

Finding the courage to break away from the person you want to be with for the rest of your life is a shattering experience. I did not think I would survive the emotional turmoil my body and mind were going through. Yet, I knew it had to be done.

So much for personal resolve. After having said many times that I would never date a married man, I had done the very thing I had tried to avoid.

I went to bed wishing my spiritual friend would come to me, and as time stood still, I went into my familiar trance state. When I awoke the next morning, the peace I felt convinced me I had been in touch with my guardian. The message I was left with was that I needed the experience to learn the lesson that we must not judge others because we are all taken in by deceivers. It restored the confidence I needed to carry on.

I now felt the need to meditate regularly after that. As I meditated one night, I was told that we are all born with a natural instinct that triggers the divine voice within us. We know it as our intuition. When we consciously develop our spiritual side, our intuition is the source that helps us make the right decisions in our lives. With free will, we are allowed to make mistakes, but with divine help, we are led to think about the right choices. It took me a while to fully comprehend this great knowledge, but with practice, I noticed that it really worked. It became the conscious path I wanted to follow the rest of my life.

* * *

The next time Mr. Burnstein came to town, he informed me he had purchased a two-story building on one of the side streets only two blocks from our current location. The building had two floors. The first floor would feature a men's apparel shop. The entire second floor would be the new ladies' boutique. It was large enough to have a private office plus a huge storage room. We spent nearly a month getting settled into our new building. This was a hectic and involved period for me. My duties were expanded to ordering all the items we carried, and keeping up with the inventory was mindboggling. I found myself on the phone with the New York wholesale houses for hours on a daily basis.

I was given permission to hire a new girl, and after several interviews, I selected the one named Jeanette. She had retail experience and would be easy to train, and later I made her my assistant. We eventually hired more girls to keep up with the volume of business. After being open only two weeks, it was evident the store was an instant success. Our old customers came in frequently and brought their friends in. We now ran ads in the local newspaper, and our sales soared even more. Without my having to ask, Mr. Burnstein gave me a raise. I was content and happier than I had been in a long time.

* * *

While I was at work one Monday, the phone rang. It was my sister Terry. She sounded very excited and asked me to come to her apartment after work. She had a big surprise for me, reminding me that it was my twenty-second birthday. The excitement in her voice made it sound pretty enticing, so I told her I would come as soon as I could after closing the store. My curiosity worked on me all day long, and I could not wait for the day to end, wondering what the big surprise was. She and her family had moved to an apartment in town a few months before. It was walking distance from the store. I arrived at her apartment in the shortest time possible, feeling tired but flushed with anticipation. I was surprised when I walked into the living room to see my mother and my brother Emile with his wife. Terry followed me into the room, and as I looked around, I saw they were all grinning, waiting for my reaction. Sitting in the corner was a man I had never seen before. I stood feeling foolish as they began singing "Happy Birthday." The silence that followed was disquieting, and I finally asked, "Well, where is the big surprise you told me about?"

Everyone looked at each other and grinned. Terry finally spoke. "Do you know who that man sitting in the corner is?"

Looking him over carefully, I replied, "Heavens, no! I've never seen him before in my life. Who is he anyway?"

The man stood up and came towards me with his arms outstretched. A gleam entered his eyes, and a big smile flashed on his face, as he announced, "Hello Lucille. I am your father. I have waited a long time for this moment."

I recoiled as if a snake was ready to attack me. I screamed and called him a son of a bitch, telling him not to come any closer. A tirade of every swear word I had ever heard followed. My insults continued, and I shouted, "I do not have a father! I never had a father!"

My anger was beyond control. I lashed out at him with all the pent-up hatred and resentment I had been harboring all of my life.

"It's one thing to plant a seed, but if you don't nurture it and help it to grow, you cannot claim it as yours," I said. "Where were you when I was sick? Where were you when we needed food, clothing, or a hug? Where were you when we were mistreated in the convent? And why did you leave our mother bruised and bleeding in the snow when she was pregnant with Emile, your third child? Did you give a damn back then about what would happen to her, or to us? I think not, you selfish bastard. You are not a father, certainly not my father. How dare you come into our lives now that we are adults and don't need you. Get out of my sight. I never want to see you again!"

Sadly, since he and Mother had never divorced because they were Catholic, she allowed him to move back in with her. Within days, she saw that he had not changed. He pranced back and forth in the house like a man on the run, chain-smoking cigarettes and always looking out the window facing the street below. His behavior was most suspicious. After two weeks of this, Mother could no longer tolerate his obnoxious ways and ordered him to leave. She threatened to turn him over to the police if he did not go quietly. He left in the middle of the night a few days later, and I never saw him again. Terry, on the other hand, visited him in New York a few times over the course of many years. But I never had the desire to know him.

The occasion of meeting my father for the first time as an adult opened my eyes. It helped me to understand why my mother had placed us in a convent when I was so young. With three children, it was her only choice. I loved her even more when I understood the sacrifices she was forced to make.

11

MEETING ART

In June of 1950, the United States pledged to give all necessary military and economic aid to the Republic of South Korea in the face of the Communist attacks from North Korea. When North Korea crossed the 38th parallel and escalated their attacks on South Korea, President Truman pledged that the U.S. would support South Korea and gave General Douglas MacArthur the authority to commit American infantry units to help the United Nation's troops defend South Korea. That October, the Communist Party took over Peking, in the People's Republic of China. America was involved in another war.

On July 7, 1950, the U.S. government implemented the draft again, and many of our young men were drafted into active duty. The qualified reservists from World War II were recalled to active duty. Since this was mostly a ground war, infantrymen were needed desperately. The South Koreans had poorly trained men and no anti-tank weapons. They needed our help to stop the Communists from taking over their country.

Everybody was aware that this war would affect their lives, but there wasn't anything we could do to prevent it. We went about our daily routines almost oblivious to what was happening in Korea.

As the war escalated in Korea, the military bases that had closed after World War II began to reopen. The air base in my hometown, Grenier AFB, was one of them. I saw advertisements in the newspaper for job openings in the Base Exchange daily. My attention was drawn to them several times, and I did not know why. I liked my job and was happy where I was.

One Monday, out of the blue, I decided to take the day off and left Jeanette in charge. By midmorning, I finished my house cleaning and began thinking about what I should do with the rest of my day. I took a shower and put on a new navy blue suit. As if a hand was pushing me, I found myself walking the few blocks to the bus stop and boarding the bus going to Grenier Air Force Base. It was a thirty-minute ride, and as we rolled along, I decided to apply for a job at the base exchange. It was as if the idea had been planted in my mind. This was indeed divine intervention, as I later discovered.

When the bus pulled up in front of the gated entrance, the bus driver told us he could not drive inside the base. We would have to walk the rest of the way. Living in town, I seldom went out in the countryside. Since the temperature was in the mid eighties, the three-quarter-mile walk to the base exchange was invigorating. I entered the BX and asked the girl at the front desk where to apply for a job. She directed me to the personnel office in the back of the room.

As I walked into the office, I was taken by surprise. A very small man wearing a bellhop's uniform was standing on top of one of the desks. His arms were outstretched, and he was yelling at the top of his voice in a song fashion, "Call for Philip Morris."

I found out later that it was Johnny, the mascot promoter for some new cigarettes called Philip Morris. When Johnny finished performing, he looked at me, winked, and jumped down from the desk. All the airmen swarmed around him, asking for his autograph, each one handing him a pen and whatever paper or picture they wanted him to sign. At the time, I did not know who he was, but in the following years, I saw him many times on television.

One of the airmen finally took notice of me and asked if I needed help. I explained that I had come to apply for one of the job openings. He escorted me into another room, where three officers in charge of the base personnel were busy at their desks. The airman whispered to a Captain sitting to his left. The Captain then stood up and asked if he could be of assistance. All eyes were now riveted on me. I felt conspicuous, but he quickly put me at ease by saying, "Please come here and take a seat next to my desk while I gather the information I need in order to process your job application."

The room was small, so everyone could hear our conversation. After several general questions, he asked where I had lived before, since I did not have the local New England accent. I told him I had lived in New Mexico and in New Britain, Connecticut. A Lieutenant who was sitting at a nearby desk jumped up and exclaimed, "No kidding, really? New Britain, Connecticut, is my hometown. That's where I'm from!"

We exchanged a few pleasantries, and after completing the application, I left. I was halfway back to the bus stop when I heard someone yelling, "Oh, Miss Connecticut! "

I kept walking, ignoring the caller because I did not think he meant me. When I reached the bus stop, I was tired and sweaty. I sat on the bench to wait for the bus that came every hour on the hour. Looking at my watch, I saw that it would be another twenty minutes before the bus would arrive.

A few minutes later, I saw a car approaching. It was coming from the base area and stopped directly in front of me. I immediately recognized the Lieutenant from Connecticut. He reached across the seat and yelled through the open window, "I'm going into town. Would you like a ride, since the bus won't be here for another twenty minutes?"

"No, I don't mind waiting for the bus. But thanks anyway," I said.

He drove off and disappeared around a bend in the road. Some minutes later, he came back and pulled up in front of the gate again, saying, "Listen, the bus won't be here for a while. In fact, they have been known to run late. I really would like to get to know you better. Since we both lived in New Britain, we may even know some of the same people." I again refused.

It was now five minutes past the hour, with no bus in sight. The next time he came by and asked, I got into his car. He acted like a gentleman, and since he was an officer in the air force, I decided I could trust him. On the way into town, we talked about Connecticut and where I had lived, compared to where his mother and father lived. He was really excited to meet someone he could talk to about the familiar places of his childhood. He even knew a cousin of mine who lived there. We talked as if we had known each other for many years.

Before I had gotten into his car, he introduced himself as Art Edgarian, but added that everybody called him "Ace," explaining that it was because of an incident that occurred during World War II.

When we arrived in town, he asked if I would join him for a drink. He suggested a fashionable cozy bar he had been to several times and told me it was a very nice place, where we would be able to continue our conversation. I had begun enjoying myself and wanted to get to know him better, so I accepted his offer. We did not run out of things to talk about, and our excitement increased when we discovered we were mutually acquainted with several people, like a dentist and several shopkeepers.

We lingered over several drinks and ate complimentary peanuts. Eventually, I told him I had to leave and asked him to take me home. Instead, he insisted I join him for dinner in the adjoining dining room. We ordered steak dinners with a salad, while carrying on a stimulating conversation. It was wonderful, being with a man who was intelligent and seemed interested in me.

Since it was the month of June, it was still daylight when we emerged from the dimly lit dining room. As we approached his car, he asked for directions to my apartment, and within five minutes, we were at my door. After opening the door for me, he politely shook my hand and said he had a wonderful time. Before saying goodnight, he asked for my phone number at work, and I gladly gave it to him. I had listened to my intuition that day, something I had ignored doing many times before. It all seemed incredible to me that in following my intuition, I had met a most interesting man.

It was too late to visit Linda when I returned home, so I kicked off my shoes and lay on the couch. With my eyes shut, I relived the day's events in my mind's eye, thinking back about how I had met Art. I remembered noticing him behind his desk and was drawn to his exceptional blue violet eyes and dark curly hair. He was quite handsome, but older. I estimated he must be in his early thirties, as his hair was receding from his forehead. He was of medium height with a muscular build.

On the way into town, he had shared his life story with me. He told me he had been a bombardier attached to a B-29 squadron during World War II. On one of their bombing missions over Germany, the plane was hit above France, and the entire crew had to abandon the plane. Luckily, they parachuted to safety. The crew had to separate for safety and security reasons, and each person was responsible for finding his way to an allied base in England on their own. Being a top-secret mission, no one was to talk about his whereabouts or how they got there. The mission was hailed a success because the targets Art had bombed were crucial to the war effort.

After many weeks of being lost and using the survival tactics he had been taught, Art found help to reach England, where he was immediately taken to a hospital. His wounds were badly infected, and he was required to remain in the hospital for more than eight months. The hospital staff nicknamed him "Ace" for his daring escape and rescue. While in the hospital, he was not allowed to contact his parents. Unfortunately, Art had been reported killed in action when he was unaccounted for, and during the months he spent in the hospital, his family and friends believed he was dead. The local newspaper featured his story on the front page, declaring him killed in action. The family was devastated and even held a funeral for him.

While he recuperated in England, the air force changed his status to missing in action. When he was finally released from the hospital and sent home, he was greeted not only as a hero but one who had returned from the dead. Imagine the celebration the town held in his honor when he returned home! He had a box full of medals and citations that our government bestows on its war heroes for wounds and bravery during combat.

After the war, he finished his college education with the help of the G.I. Bill at the University of Connecticut. He received his degree in political science and personnel management. He told me that while in school he had married his college sweetheart, but after two years, they reached a mutual agreement to divorce.

He was recalled back into the air force when the war broke out in Korea and was assigned to Grenier AFB, as a Personnel Officer. In one day, Art told me a great deal about himself. His openness about his past told me he could be trusted and that he was extremely honest.

That night, as I lay in bed with my eyes shut, I could not help but think that we *do* have control over our lives. It all depends on the decisions we choose to make. I could have stayed home all day. I could have decided not to take the bus. I could have decided not to accept a ride with Art, and I could have chosen not to give him my phone number. I was aware that I had followed my intuition by listening to the voice within and had followed its guidance.

When I picked up Linda for the weekend, Mrs. Goslin tearfully greeted me by saying she was not well, and she would not be able to care for Linda any longer. I would have to make other arrangements as soon as possible. Sadness overwhelmed me when she told me of her illness, especially when I learned she had cancer, with no hope of a cure. I couldn't believe that this would spell the end of a wonderful life. I had grown to love Mrs. Goslin. She was like an extended member of my family, closer than an aunt could be, and her daughters had become like my nieces. Luckily, her daughters were in high school now and would be able to take care of their mother. I truly hated to see our relationship end. It had been so perfect. I knew it was going to be hard to replace the only home Linda had known since infancy. How I dreaded facing the changes I would have to make. I left with a heavy heart.

While riding the bus home, I began thinking about an added problem I had not expected. Finding a suitable place for Linda was not going to be easy and would take time. Focusing on my divine source, I nightly asked for advice, and ideas began to form in my mind. It took several weeks of searching and inquiring. Then, an acquaintance told me about a Presbyterian Church that had live-in accommodations for children. It sounded like the type of place I was looking for.

The following Monday during my lunch break, I walked to the school unannounced. I wanted to see how the children were being cared for and to see if they appeared to be happy. Making several more unexpected visits, I found that the staff always greeted me warmly and the children were always involved in supervised play. Often, someone would be reading to them. One day I stayed for lunch, and on another visit, I stayed for dinner. I found the food was always well balanced and excellent. The dining room had low round tables for the children, with four to six chairs around each one. It was the cutest set-up I had ever seen.

Even the large bedrooms on the second floor were neat and nicely arranged. Each bedroom accommodated children in a certain age group. The room that Linda would be assigned to was large, with small beds along several walls and large spaces next to each bed for the child's individual possessions and toys. I could picture Linda's baby carriage, dolls, and stuffed animals placed around the bed, making it like home for her. The best part was the location, a mere four blocks from where I worked. The cost was more than what I had been paying Mrs. Goslin, but it was affordable.

Considering it included preschool classes, I felt it was reasonable. After weeks of searching, I knew I had found the perfect home for my little girl and enrolled her. I felt I had been led there because the solution turned out to be a perfect and effortless transition.

Art tried calling me at work ever since the first day we met. I had been so busy with finding a place for Linda to live that I had to turn down his invitations to join him for dinner several times. About three weeks after our first meeting, he called again. This time his message was brief. In a firm voice, he told me he would be waiting for me in front of the store when I got off work, and he did not want to hear any excuses.

"I will take you out for dinner where we can talk without any interruptions. After that, if you decide you don't want to see me again, I will honor your decision and leave you alone. I promise I will never try to contact you again."

I was ready for some socializing and agreed to have dinner with him. As I closed the store for the night, his car pulled up in front. My heart skipped a beat, and I sensed this was the beginning of a new phase in my life. Over dinner, I told him I had a child and filled him in on the latest news about Linda. I felt if he did not want to be involved with me because I had a child, this would give him the opportunity to stop calling me. During the meal he surprised me by saying he was thrilled to hear about my daughter and wanted to know when he could meet her. He asked how old she was and wanted to know if I had a picture of her. Of course, I gladly produced one from my purse. He exclaimed how adorable and cute she was. His enthusiasm was genuine, and I felt much more comfortable with him during the course of the evening.

We arranged to meet the following night, after I got off work. As we drove to Mrs. Goslin's house, Art squeezed my hand and turned to smile at me, saying how happy he was. After parking the car, he reached over and kissed me. By now, I was pleased to see he was genuinely interested in me, that I was not just a passing fancy.

When I introduced Linda to Art, she ran to him and allowed him to pick her up. He hugged her and kissed her on the cheek. She put her little arms around his neck and nuzzled her face into it. Tears welled in my eyes as I saw this. She had never shown this much affection to a male person before. I could see that Art was overjoyed at her reaction to him. Before we left, I arranged to pick up Linda the following Friday evening and told Mrs. Goslin I would be taking all her possessions at that time. It would be my last visit to her home.

I spent the weekend telling Linda about the wonderful school I had found and that I would be taking her there soon. I tried to make her understand that she would have many playmates who would become her new friends.

The following Friday, I took Linda to the school to let her get acquainted with the teachers and the staff. As we walked into the various rooms, I told her this was where she was going to live for a while, and she was not going back to Mrs. Goslin's house anymore. She did not seem upset, but since she was three years old, I don't know how much she really understood. The children came running to greet her, and one little girl in particular, named Lisa, came over and hugged her.

When Sunday arrived, I was nervous about taking Linda to her new home. Art helped me pack all her things in his car, and we drove the short distance to the Presbyterian school. Linda was really excited about going back to see her new friend Lisa. We were greeted warmly at the door and spent the next hour bringing in Linda's belongings. After carefully arranging everything in her assigned drawers, I placed her doll carriage with its precious cargo next to her bed, just as I had visualized it. We were asked to stay for dinner and agreed, in order to make Linda feel at home. I especially wanted to see how she would adjust to her new surroundings.

We sat at Linda's little table with some of the children. They talked and giggled, and I could see she felt very much at home. When the time came for Art and me to leave, Linda came running to me, wrapped her arms around my neck, and planted kisses all over my face. Then she said goodbye. Art picked her up and received his share of kisses as well. As soon as he set her down, like most children, she could not run fast enough to rejoin her new friend Lisa. That was the best sign I could have asked for. It assured me I had made the right decision. I felt comfortable in knowing she was in caring hands, with people who would learn to love her like Mrs. Goslin and her girls had.

For the next seven months, Art joined me at least two nights per week to visit Linda. The school encouraged the parents to visit in the evening after dinner for an hour. Art also attended all her plays and other special events during various holidays. I was thrilled to know that Linda was in the best place I could have found. She was kept busy during the week, and on weekends, she would be with me from Friday afternoon until Sunday evening.

The most memorable event that took place while she was at the school was a Christmas play that Linda participated in. We both beamed with pride as she went through her small speaking role. I must say she looked beautiful in her bright red taffeta dress with red ribbons in her hair. She was so cute and funny, turning and waving to us from the stage. The entire room broke out laughing at her cute antics. Art was as proud as I was to see her perform. Later in the program, when she joined the choir in singing Christmas songs, Art took my hand in his, overcome by the emotion that had built up in him. I looked at him and I saw a tear run down his cheek

The following months were the most carefree and fun-filled days I could ever have wished for. Being an officer in the air force gave Art a lot of authority and privileges. As a personnel officer, he held an important position that brought him much respect from the other officers, as well as the enlisted personnel and civilian workers on the base. As his girlfriend, I was treated like a queen, with almost regal respect.

The Officers' Club was the meeting place for all functions, and on Friday nights, it was the place to gather for formal dining as well as dancing. Art and I joined the other officers and their wives on those festive evenings, and after dinner, we danced the entire evening away, accompanied by live bands that were famous at the time. I was overjoyed to have found someone who also enjoyed my favorite pastime. Being young, we were filled with excitement as we danced and partied. This new lifestyle was made possible because, whenever Art and I went out, Mother insisted on taking care of Linda, who always looked forward to spending the night with her grandmother.

As the weeks went by, Art and I talked about our past and began understanding each other more. He told me he was Armenian and how the Armenian people took great pride in their country, which dated back thousands of years. I had never even heard of Armenia and was intrigued to hear about their culture. As our love deepened, Art decided to call his mother to tell her about me. He passed the phone to me, and while we talked, I found his mother was polite but cautious. Wanting to please her son, she ended our conversation by inviting me to visit them with Art soon. That's when I knew he was serious about me because most Armenians did not readily accept a non-Armenian into the family.

As soon as we both had a free weekend, we drove to Connecticut. I was surprised to find that his parents lived in an apartment not far from where I had lived six years before. On our second night, his mom and dad invited other family members and friends to drop in to see Art and meet his girlfriend. As they began arriving, I was sure they had come to check out the non-Armenian girl that Art had fallen in love with.

During the evening, Art decided to let them all know I had been married before and was divorced. He quickly informed them that I had a three-year-old daughter named Linda. I know my face turned red and my hands began shaking from the nervous tension because I had not expected that revelation to be made so soon.

The silence that followed was unnerving, to say the least. I expected to be told to forget Art and move on, that my type was not accepted. But to my surprise, no one seemed upset by the news. It had taken time for them to absorb what they heard. Like a floodgate had opened, they all began talking at once. In fact, they showed genuine friendship towards me, and one by one invited me to visit them the next time we were in town. Before leaving, each person told me they were looking forward to meeting my daughter.

After that initial visit, Art and I visited his family often and always brought Linda along. Everyone looked forward to the opportunity to get to know us better, and we formed a close relationship with the entire family. I now had an extended family, and Linda looked forward to the attention they paid her.

During our courtship, Art and I developed a close friendship with another couple named Mavis and Scott. They lived on the base in one of the converted barracks. The entire second floor was their apartment. It was so huge that they occupied only one end of it. They had a daughter a few months older than Linda and a son who was one year younger. They always wanted us to bring Linda when we came because, while the children played, it gave us the freedom to visit and play our own favorite games. Many weeknights, other friends joined us to play canasta or poker. Mavis and some of the other ladies made dips and serve snacks I had never tasted before, and I was introduced to the social side of life that couples shared, a new experience for me.

Several months after Art and I had been seriously dating, Mavis and Scott told us they wanted to get away for a few days and asked if we would mind babysitting for them. Since it was a long holiday weekend and we didn't have any other plans, we were more than happy to.

The first day was hectic. I was not used to watching three rambunctious children run around. I was exhausted but thrilled when they went to bed and fell asleep early. Art and I decided to relax on the couch and began kissing, then fondling, each other. After months of abstinence, we could no longer hold back. Our longing for each other reached a feverish pitch. After that night, nothing could keep us apart. His passion for me matched my own for him.

A few months later, Art called me from work to say he needed to talk to me as soon as possible. It involved a complicated new development. It sounded serious. I wondered what had happened. I was anxious for the day to end so I could find out what was so earth shaking. Art arrived soon after I got home and didn't say a word for a long time. He just watched while I prepared dinner in silence. I knew he was upset and didn't know how to approach the subject. My stomach tightened up in knots with fear of the bad news I knew he was holding back. After the dishes were cleaned and put away, we sat on the living room couch. Taking my hand in his, Art began telling me the news.

"I received orders today that I am being transferred to Brooklyn College in Brooklyn, New York. I have been assigned to be an ROTC instructor. I have to leave in two weeks and report to duty."

"Oh, my God," I managed to get out of my constricted throat, "Does this mean that you are leaving for good and we will not see each other anymore? The thought of losing you is almost more than I can bear."

"I need a few days to think about what to do. This is so unexpected, and I need time to think," he responded.

"Of course you do," I said, "Our future depends on your decision."

Taking me in his arms, he began crying, repeating, "I'm so afraid to make a commitment at this time. I really don't want to lose you, yet I don't want to make another mistake, so I need some time to think this through."

What could I say?

After spending a sleepless night, I had to force myself to go to work the next morning. I stayed busy all day to make the time go by faster. When six o'clock came, I was reluctant to leave the store, wanting time to freeze, afraid to face the possibility that Art might not come to get me. With a heavy heart, I went outside and spotted his car approaching. He parked in front of the store, jumped out of the car, ran to me, picked me up off the ground, and swung me around. In a voice loud enough for the entire neighborhood to hear, he shouted, "Will you marry me? Please say yes. I cannot go through life without you. I love you and Linda so much. You are such a wonderful mother to her, and I want you to be the mother of my children as well."

I hugged him as hard as I could and kissed him repeatedly. Being all out of breath I managed to say, "Of course I'll marry you! There is no way I would let you walk out of my life. We are part of each other now. Without you, my life has no meaning."

We quickly got into his car and went to my apartment. After running up the flight of stairs, Art ran to the phone and called his parents. They were thrilled to hear the news and said they were very happy for us. His mother asked to speak with me. She expressed her love for me and Linda, and assured me the entire family felt the way she did. My intuition told me Art had discussed his decision with his parents before coming to his own conclusion.

* * *

The world took on a new glow for me as I became involved with plans for our wedding. Since we did not have much time to plan a big wedding, we agreed to be married in the Armenian Church in New York City. The Armenian Bishop who had been a family friend for many years would perform the ceremony. Art's sister Kanare took care of all the details because she lived in New Jersey, an easy commute into New York City. I personally would not have known what to do.

The next week flew by with so much to do. I told my mother the great news, and she was thrilled but sad that I would be leaving. Having Linda away was going to be hard for her to get used to. She added she was not surprised; she knew it was only a matter of time before Art would ask me to marry him.

Kanare invited Mother and Linda to stay at their house the entire time the wedding took place. Since the reception would be at their house following the ceremony, she insisted they stay as long as necessary afterwards—even during the time that Art and I were on our honeymoon and for the extended period we would need to locate a place to live in Brooklyn, Mother and Linda stayed with them. Kanare had two daughters and a son who became great playmates for Linda.

My mind was whirling with the many changes taking place in my life, and the good fortune that everything was being solved for me so easily. With only two weeks to prepare that included several trips to New Jersey, the days just flew by. Within a week, all the plans were finalized. That is when I decided to tell Mr. Burnstein I was leaving.

On Monday morning when Mr. Burnstein came in, I told him I needed to have a serious talk with him. We went to his office and I told him I was getting married. I said I had only a few days left before I would be moving out of the state. He was surprised, and I tried to lighten the shock by suggesting that he put Jeanette in charge. I had trained her well and knew she was ready to assume my role as manager. He thanked me for a job well done and added that he would miss me very much. I left there feeling liberated.

I learned later from one of Jeanette's letters that the store was closing. She told me the men's department had been draining all the profits from the ladies' department for over a year. Even though Mr. Burnstein had tried to keep it profitable while I was there, he realized it had become a losing proposition. She told me they had a going-out-of-business sale, and Mr. Burnstein went back to Massachusetts to concentrate on his other stores. It dawned on me as I read her letter that my days as store manager would have ended anyway had I stayed. What a strange coincidence, I thought. By responding to my intuition, I met Art and was entering a life change.

Kanare had been busy making all the arrangements for our wedding—securing the Bishop, reserving the church, ordering the flowers, getting the singers, and having all the food prepared by the Armenian women in their church. Her big gorgeous house would accommodate nearly all the out-of-town guests, she told me, including her parents, Mr. and Mrs. Edgarian, Linda, Mother, several aunts and uncles, plus Art and me.

The Armenian wedding ceremony lasted nearly two hours. Kanare was my matron of honor, and her husband Vigen was the best man. The church was packed with friends from all over the country. I had no idea how many friends Art had, so I was surprised when close to one hundred showed up. Following the ceremony, we all gathered at Vigen and Kanare's house for an incredible reception.

I was shocked when I saw the wedding gifts. They covered a huge banquet size table. They included a silver place setting for twelve, a beautiful silver coffee serving set with a matching tray, and a china service for twelve from Germany. Other gifts included pots and pans of every size and just about everything else needed for the kitchen and bathroom. It was unbelievable that this was happening to me.

Toasting the bride and groom went on for an hour. We drank, and ate the delicious Armenian delicacies that the ladies of the church had prepared. It was a feast like no other, one I certainly had never witnessed before. I felt like I had been transported to a fairyland and was a princess in another world.

By eleven p.m., Art and I were exhausted and asked to be excused. We hugged and exchanged pleasantries with everyone, and then left for our honeymoon. The long drive took an hour before we arrived at our destination. Luckily, Art had made reservations at a motel along the way, and by the time we cleaned up and got into bed, we were so tired, we both fell asleep.

The following day, we woke up refreshed and ready for the busy day ahead. The drive to Brooklyn was interesting, since I had never been there before. We spent several hours looking for a place to move into. By midday, we succeeded in finding a small basement apartment, fully furnished on

Dekalb Avenue, not far from Brooklyn College, where Art was going to work.

We returned to New Jersey several days later and spent the weekend visiting with the remaining relatives who were still at Kanare's house. I was disappointed to learn that my mother had left the day before. Linda had missed me terribly and ran into my arms when she saw me.

* * *

On Monday, Art and I gathered all our belongings, and with Linda in tow, headed for our new home in Brooklyn. Art had been serious when he told me he did not want me to work anymore. He wanted me to be a stay-at-home mom and devote all my time to Linda. Most of all, he looked forward to my being home to greet him when he arrived home after work. My dream of being a family and having Linda with me all the time had miraculously happened. I could not have been happier.

Art reported to work the following week, and after being briefed on his new assignment, officially became an instructor of political science in the ROTC program. Several weeks later, the other ROTC instructors and their wives gave us a welcoming party. It was held in one of their homes on Long Island, New York. We were told they lived in close proximity of each other to make it convenient for them to carpool to work every day. This enabled them to save on gas and took care of the limited parking space on campus. There were six other officers besides Art in the ROTC program, making them an exclusive group.

Much to my delight, the wives were extremely friendly and accepted me immediately. Before long, we found we enjoyed each other's company and became close friends. Each one was eager to help and wanted to explain my new role as an officer's wife. They informed me there were many rules and regulations to follow. They warned me that the top ranking officers and their wives watched a wife's behavior very closely. They stressed that I had to familiarize myself with protocol, since it affected my husband's chances of getting promoted.

Officers' wives were expected to join the officers' wives club and participate in all their activities. Business meetings were held once a month. The base commander would make a special appearance in order to welcome the new wives as members. Guest speakers discussed interesting subjects at every meeting. Some were selected to keep us informed about our duties and responsibilities. These monthly meetings were mandatory.

The base commander's wife was regarded as the official "First Lady" on the base, and she presided at all the meetings. We held her in high esteem and looked up to her as an example. There was an elected board of officers that consisted of a president, first, second, and third vice presidents, a treasurer, and a secretary. These meetings taught us how to conduct business following Robert's Rules of Order.

As officers' wives, we were encouraged to be proud of our status and to be well groomed at all times. When in public, we represented the United States Air Force. We had discussions on how to dress properly, and we wore hats and gloves to all the afternoon functions. Occasionally, they promoted style shows and invited some of the wives to participate as models. The formal luncheons and teas taught us how to act while we dined. We also learned the proper way to address and greet people.

Once a month, there was a formal dance honoring either the base commander and his wife or a visiting dignitary. This was another command performance we were expected to attend. If you did not attend, your husband would have to report to his superior and explain why. They expected a good reason because it could directly affect his career and a chance for promotion.

The formal dances were the most elegant and wonderful events of the year. The Officers' Club was decorated in a theme befitting the occasion. The officers wore their dress uniforms of white jackets ablaze with the medals they had accumulated during their respective careers. Their black pants and white hats trimmed in black made for a very impressive appearance. The ladies wore long formal gowns and long white gloves to the elbow at these events. Every woman stood out as a beauty. I looked forward to those formal gatherings because they truly captured the essence of a Cinderella night.

As our husbands rose in rank, we were kept aware that our turn might come one day to be the wife of the Base Commander. This prospect kept us on our toes, and we took our roles seriously. During my years with the air force, I learned that many First Ladies were extremely nice. Others, however, were inclined to be snobbish, cold, and calculating. A few were mean-spirited. I learned an important fact: A person's personality does not change when they reach the top.

The top-ranking officers' wives did not mingle with the low-ranking officers' wives. Unless one of them sought you out, you did not dare assume you were equals. As a new wife, I had a lot to learn. "Rank has its privileges" was an often-repeated slogan. The separation of ranks was discriminating, I know, but it was a rule accepted by all the military branches.

* * *

Being a full-time housewife was a dream come true. I took to the role like a duck to water. Our basement apartment in the heart of Brooklyn had a small enclosed yard in the back, with enough room to have a playground for Linda. We were able to enjoy the outdoors in privacy, and when the sun was shining, we could actually bask in it for a while.

My days were spent going for walks with Linda and shopping at the local meat market or bakery. Standing in line with all the women shouting their demands at the butcher or the baker was quite an experience. I had never seen this type of behavior before. It was not only "first come, first serve," but also who yelled the loudest. The first few times I encountered this, I was timid. I stood patiently, waiting for my turn at the butcher shop.

One day, and after waiting for quite some time, the butcher yelled, "Hey, lady. If ya want some meat, ya better yell it out loud like the rest of 'em; otherwise, you're gonna be here all day!"

After that, I began yelling my order as soon as I walked in the door, just like the others. It felt strange, but I soon got used to it because it was the only way to get served. I learned to fit in with the local customs in no time.

To pass the time one day, I took Linda to the nearby public library. This became such a favorite pastime that we began spending several days a week in the library, feasting on the endless rows of books. After awhile, Linda knew where all her favorite books were, and she picked her own books to read that day. Before leaving, she selected the ones she wanted to take home. After her nap, it was my time to read to her. Reading was our most enjoyable pastime, and I know it instilled a love for books in her that she never lost.

I made up stories from my imagination because Linda used to say, "Mommy, tell me a story from your head."

As I made up stories, I changed my voice to mimic each character. Linda loved it, and she rolled with laughter or was frightened at the evil characters and hid behind my skirt. Our make-believe times kept us so busy that the time went by fast. Next thing we knew, it was time for Art to come home, and we had to hurry to pick up our mess.

Being home full time gave me the opportunity to experiment with cooking as well. I found that I enjoyed preparing great meals. My favorites were still the Greek dishes I had learned to make from Ernie's mother. Now I was making newly learned Armenian dishes. Many were quite similar, like stuffed grape leaves, baklava, pilaf, and lamb stew, to name a few. I made certain we had a balanced meal every night that always included a salad and a dessert. Having been deprived as a child, I wanted my family to be well fed.

After being in Brooklyn for nearly three months, I suspected one morning that I was pregnant. Art was overjoyed when I told him, as we got ready for bed that night. He immediately began talking about buying a house on Long Island, where we would be close to his coworkers. There were so many new subdivisions that it was difficult to decide where to look. After spending two months looking intensively, we found our dream home in East Meadow. It was a lovely Cape Cod design with plenty of room.

Just the idea that we were considering buying a house frightened me. When I heard the price was eleven thousand dollars, it scared me so badly that my heart began to pound. It was more money than I could imagine us owing, and I was convinced it would put us in debt for the rest of our lives. Art laughed and quickly eased my concerns by saying that with his Veteran status, we could buy the house with nothing down. With a thirty-year mortgage, our monthly payments would be well within our means. I was shocked when I realized how much the price of homes had gone up since the one Ernie and I had purchased in Albuquerque in 1947.

Three weeks later, after all the paperwork was finalized, we closed on the house. At the end of the week, we happily moved into our new home with the help of our many friends. While the loan was being processed, we had shopped for the furniture we would need. Amazingly, the money we had received as wedding gifts was enough to pay for all the furniture, a new refrigerator, plus a new washer and dryer. I had never owned so many things in my life. In my mind, I was still the poor little girl who had been raised in dire poverty. This was like a fairytale. Was my guardian creating this incredible change as a lesson to compare later in my life?

After two days, Linda made friends with the boy next door named Phillip, along with several other children on our street. She was one happy little girl, having her own bedroom for the first time. Being a precocious five-year-old, she arranged her many dolls and stuffed animals in rows, while pretending to be their mommy. She spent hours playing imaginary games with them. Our time spent together was even more fun now as we cooked, cleaned, and did things that had been impossible before. We talked about the baby that was coming to prepare Linda for a new little brother or sister.

Lucille and Theresa
in convent uniforms in 1934

Lucille
in confirmation dress in 1941

Edgarian family in Italy. From back left: Art,
Linda, Lucille. From front left: Debbie and Arty

Professor Pio Rossi

Art and Lucille – 1963, at Randolph
Air Force Base, San Antonio

Lucille, President, San Antonio Chapter,
National Society of Arts and Letters,
1981–82

Lucille and Bill, Austin, Texas, 2005

Texas Topaz with Bluebonnets, Painting by Lucille

12

ARTISTIC AWAKENING

As the due date approached, the doctor decided to induce labor one week early, in case the baby might be Rh-positive. As it turned out, the baby had Rh-negative blood, like me, and did not need to have the transfusions that Linda had suffered through. What a relief that was. Art came to see me every day and could not contain his pleasure as he gazed at his beautiful new daughter.

We decided to name our new baby Debbie. I was ecstatic the day the nurse brought her to me for the first time. I marveled at God's perfect creation, a baby girl born with such a pink glow and black curly hair. I was surprised that a mother's heart could hold so much love, that it was possible to feel the same strong love for the new being in my arms as I felt for Linda.

Being five years old, Linda treated Debbie as if she were her own new doll and became very attached to her. It was wonderful to watch them together, and seeing Linda embrace the role of big sister was amazing. She became a big help to me in caring for her baby sister. Before long, we were a threesome and did everything together.

When Debbie turned six months old, we had a lavish baptism for her. It took place in the Armenian Church in New York City where we had been married. Armenian families treat a baptism as a very special event, and relatives came from many states to take part in this festive occasion. The ceremony lasted for over an hour, with the old traditions and formalities that took place. Afterwards we gathered at Kanare's house in New Jersey, where the party lasted all day.

The lavish gifts we received were unbelievable. Quite a few relatives gave cash; others made sure we received all the equipment and necessities a new mother would need. I did not have to buy a thing for my baby. She even received a silver spoon and silver cup. Like the old saying, she was born with a silver spoon in her mouth!

As blonde as Linda was, Debbie was the extreme opposite. Her hair was jet black, like Art's, with small ringlets. When it grew longer, it became a mass of curls. Debbie was such a good baby. She seldom cried. She smiled all the time, very much like Linda had when she was a baby. By the time Debbie turned two years old, her hair had lightened, and she looked very much like Shirley Temple, the little movie star. As a stay-at-home mom, I was able to enjoy the progress that Debbie made, but it saddened me to realize how much I had missed out on during those important phases in Linda's early years.

* * *

A few years after settling into our new routines in New York, I began experiencing my old desire to paint. My dream of becoming an artist had never died, and now it became an obsession. Painting was all I thought about, and I couldn't shake it. As the yearning consumed me, I decided to let my intuition take over. One night, as Art and I lay in bed talking about our day, I told him of my deep yearning to take art lessons. To my surprise, he said he knew how much that meant to me and remembered my telling him when we first met that becoming an artist was my life's ambition. With his full support, I began inquiring about schools in the area that offered art classes. Within two weeks, I was enrolled in a night class four nights per week.

My instructor, Miss Cole, was a young woman in her twenties. She was rather tall and wore Ben Franklin-type glasses giving her the appearance of an intellect that made her stand out in any gathering. Miss Cole, I discovered, had definite leanings toward being a free spirit.

Her choice of expression in art was in abstract form or cubism, using oil paints on large canvases. She preferred all forms of modern art and encouraged, or I should say, steered her students into becoming modern painters like herself. During my first class, she pretty much ignored me.

Being a brand new student who didn't know what to do, I waited patiently to be told. After awhile, it dawned on me that I better speak up. The next time she walked by me, I stopped her and asked her to give me a list of the materials I needed to buy since I was a beginner. She was visibly annoyed by my boldness, and after a deep sigh, wrote out a list of supplies I would need if I wanted to continue in her class.

The following night, I arrived with a canvas and the paints she had recommended, ready to start my new adventure. I could scarcely hide my excitement. My exuberance was short-lived because Miss Cole continued to ignore me. The girl working next to me managed to whisper that Miss Cole had been teaching classes for three years and that she considered herself a progressive artist who "had arrived." It dawned on me that Miss Cole did not have the desire or the patience to take on a beginner. She preferred advanced students or intermediates who were interested mainly in learning abstract art. Here I was a beginner, wanting to learn the basics, and my art preference was impressionistic realism. We were like oil and water, but the craving I experienced daily to become an artist was overpowering, so I clung to my belief that I had been led to this class. With firm resolve, I decided that no matter what Miss Cole said, it would not make me drop out of her class.

During my next class, I bravely laid out my paints and art materials, ready to begin. Before the students arrived, Miss Cole had arranged a still life display for us to paint. Everyone started painting, while I stood not knowing what to do. I didn't even know the proper way to lay out the paints. Miss Cole began walking to each student to give them advice or show them how to achieve certain things. She finally came to where I was, and when she saw that I didn't even have the paints arranged on my palette, she was clearly disgusted. Angrily, she shouted, "Well, when are you going to get started?"

After she walked away, the girl next to me began giving me some advice. After that, I proceeded to draw and tried to capture what I saw. After an hour, I realized that I was not having much success in getting the brown wooden plate and fruit displayed onto my canvas. I kept on painting until the teacher clapped her hands and announced, "Okay, everyone place your canvases on the blackboard. I will go by and critique each one."

I knew my painting was not finished and was pretty bad. Putting my painting next to the others, I feared what she would say about mine. She praised several other paintings and even had glowing remarks to say about a few. When she came to mine, she stood with her hands on her hips and exclaimed, "Well, all I can say about this one is that it is very muddy."

Without a word of advice, she moved on to the next painting. Silence permeated the room. Everyone looked down at the floor, wanting to avoid eye contact with me. At that moment, I wished I could become invisible. I wondered why the instructor was so mean to me. When class was dismissed, I gathered my supplies and went out to my car. I had to sit for a while to calm down, knowing I was too upset to drive home.

Not wanting Art to see me upset, I took a deep breath and entered the house with a smile on my face. He had been waiting for me with great anticipation, curious to hear how my first art lesson had gone. I made light of it and said it went well, and then I added that I wanted to stay up for a while longer to finish the painting I had started in class. I confessed that the teacher was not pleased with my work, and I wanted to improve it. He said he understood and went to bed.

I set out my paints and canvas on the breakfast room table as soon as Art left the room. My heart was still pounding from the anger I felt at being humiliated in front of the other students. I wanted to show them I was capable of painting something that was not considered muddy. My attention was drawn to the wall facing me, and there, as if I had not seen it before, was a black tray with painted flowers in the center. It had been given to us as a wedding gift. I looked down at my muddy painting, and an idea began to form. With a sense of urgency, I began to repaint my canvas. I used my imagination to paint for the first time with an uncanny feeling of painting automatically. The time flew by, and when I decided there was nothing else I could do to the painting, I looked at the clock and discovered it was two-thirty in the morning.

The next night, as soon as I got to class, I went up front to show my painting to the teacher. I wanted her to critique it and give me some advice. She looked at me and then at the canvas. She had a bewildered look on her face and asked, "Who helped you paint that?"

I told her I had stayed up most of the night and had painted it on my own. Impressed, she commented, "If you can paint like this on your own, I advise you to keep painting without instruction. You have a natural gift that you must develop on your own. Keep it up, and don't get influenced by other artists."

That was a total surprise to me. I had not expected that kind of reaction, especially from her. I continued to attend the classes, mainly because I had paid for a full semester. I learned to mix the oil paints, and by observing the other artists, I picked up many techniques and ideas that were lessons in themselves. As usual, Miss Cole preferred to ignore me, but she was much friendlier toward me as the weeks went by. When the semester ended, I continued to paint at home whenever I had a spare moment.

During this same period, I was feeling sick in the mornings and sometimes all day long. I thought it was nerves at first, or that maybe the oil paints were making me sick. But after four months of the telltale signs, I knew I was pregnant. Unlike women who crave certain foods, painting and going to class was the craving during my pregnancy. Many years later, I saw that it had influenced the baby I was carrying. As an adult, his insatiable love of paintings took him to flea markets and garage sales, always looking to buy the next painting that made his body tremble with excitement.

Art was thrilled when I told him he would be a dad again. Of course, he hoped it would be a boy to carry on the family name, but either way, he was excited that he would have another little one to love. As the months went by and the last months of pregnancy became too hectic, I realized that I had to stop painting. I was content nonetheless because I knew I could go back to painting later, when the time was right. Linda and Debbie certainly kept me busy as we spent our days reading, playing, and enjoying the time leading to the quickly approaching birth of the new baby.

During this period, there were other important things going on that kept my mind occupied. Art had been in contact with an attorney for over a year. They had been searching for Ernie, Linda's father, all year. Since Ernie had not communicated with me for many years, Art decided he wanted to adopt Linda. He wanted her to legally be his little girl and to grow up feeling the same love he felt for Debbie. He believed it was important for them to have the same last name as well. In the four years we had been together, Art had grown to love Linda as his own, and he now wanted to be considered her real father.

During the year of inquiry, the attorney learned that Ernie was in the Philippines as a field director with the American Red Cross and doing quite well financially. It took several more frustrating months before the adoption papers were signed and approved by the courts. Ernie had not objected to the adoption; as a matter of fact, he was glad that Linda would be well cared for in a loving home. When the final papers were delivered into our hands, we cried with joy. Linda was now Art's legal daughter. That was one of the most important events that occurred during our married life. Art made me agree that we would not talk about her being adopted among our friends, and we advised our relatives to never discuss it among themselves. Art also made me promise I would never tell Linda. As the years went by, Ernie never attempted to contact us.

A week before I was due to deliver the baby, my obstetrician felt it was necessary to induce labor again because I had built up antibodies that suggested the baby might have Rh-positive blood. I had been experiencing mild labor pains for over a week without going into labor. I was admitted to the hospital, and another doctor was on duty at the time. He came to my room and explained that he was going to speed the labor along and broke my water. He did this without consulting my obstetrician or getting permission from him. Instead of going into labor, I lost all the water that would have lubricated the birth canal, and I lingered in the labor room for three days with constant mild labor pains. On the third day, a different obstetrician was on duty. After examining me, he announced that I was not ready to deliver, so he was going to get a bite to eat and would return in plenty of time. On his way out, he told the nurse he would be back shortly. Not more than fifteen minutes went by when I began having severe labor pains. I screamed for the nurse. She came running to see why I was screaming, and told me to stop, but I could not. I yelled, "Look for yourself. I can feel the baby coming out!"

When she looked under the sheet, panic registered on her face. She crossed my legs and began saying repeatedly, "Don't push. Please don't push! The doctor is gone, and I don't know what to do. I've never delivered a baby before."

She rolled me onto a gurney, held my legs together, and wheeled me down the hall toward the operating room. Thank God, at that very moment another doctor happened to be walking by, and when he assessed the situation, he knew it was critical. He ran to scrub his hands and returned to the operating room. He began shouting at the nurse, "Uncross her legs before you kill the baby!"

She then ran to get him the towels he had asked for. He placed one under me, and in a kind voice said, "Hurry and push as hard as you can!"

One grunt and the baby came bouncing out. He was blue and was not crying. The doctor worked on him for quite some time before we finally heard him cry. I was well aware that the doctor had saved my baby's life. An overwhelming feeling of gratitude filled my heart.

As I relaxed, my eyes could no longer contain the tears I had been holding back when I heard him say, "It's a boy!"

I began sobbing with relief. Boy or girl, I didn't care. Knowing that my baby was alive was all that mattered. My guardian must have been watching over me because, the next day, I learned that the doctor who happened to be in the hall when I was wheeled into the operating room was a pediatrician. The added blessing was that he would be the pediatrician who would take care of my baby boy, Arty. He formed a special bond with the baby, knowing how close we had come to losing him. Because of his difficult birth, Arty required special attention. Being in a military hospital was not an ideal situation, mainly because we were seen by different doctors all the time, and it was apparent they did not consult with each other.

In spite of his difficult birth, Arty was the picture of health. He was born with a head full of curly black hair and the most gorgeous purple-blue eyes, just like his dad. I'm sure every parent feels that same pride and love when they first gaze at their newborn. We were told that Arty did not have Rh-positive blood and that he would not have to stay in the hospital for an extended period.

However, one month after his birth, Arty developed a hernia in the groin area and had to be operated on. I feared that his difficult birth might someday cause other unexpected problems. Having a boy in an Armenian family is a big deal and is considered the greatest gift a woman can give her husband. As soon as Arty recovered from the operation, we had his christening ceremony in the Armenian Church in New York City. This spectacular event was similar to the one we had had for Debbie three years before. Likewise, the festivities went on all day, with the aunts and uncles gloating over the new heir who would carry on the family name. Again, we received gifts of money that were unimaginable, and of course, countless other gifts that provided me with all the things I needed.

Linda was eight years old when Arty was born, and as a big sister, she adored her baby brother. She wanted to take care of his every need whenever I was busy. Oftentimes I felt like Art had rescued me. He was such a loving, caring husband and a wonderful father. Best of all, his entire family could not have been kinder to me. We had formed a close bond with my in-laws and visited them often. Every summer we spent an entire week at a beach house owned by Uncle Stephen and his wife Beatrice. This was always the highlight of our summers.

Art had been in the ROTC program in Brooklyn, New York, for nearly four years when Arty was born. We anticipated that he was due for reassignment soon. The Korean War had ended, and as a result, officers who had been recalled to active duty were asked to either leave or were given the opportunity to stay in the air force as career officers. Art's commanding officer requested he decide whether he was going to stay in the military or to get out. He advised Art that he needed his decision pronto.

We discussed the pros and cons for days. It was a major decision that would affect our future for many years. After much soul-searching and countless discussions with friends and family, Art decided he wanted to stay in the air force. The die was cast. His future was now set as a career officer.

Within a month, he received orders for an assignment to French Morocco in Africa. The news terrified me. I thought we were going to the ends of the earth. Going to Africa, of all places! All I could envision were wild animals and natives running half naked with spears drawn, like in prehistoric times. I was especially frightened for the children.

We began packing our household goods, located a real estate agent, and quickly signed a contract to sell the house. The entire family had to get many immunizations to protect us from various illnesses we could possibly be exposed to. It was a busy time for all of us, but we began looking forward to the new adventures that awaited us.

13

MOVING ABROAD

By the time Art received his official papers, we were ready. He arranged to have our car shipped so it would be there shortly after we arrived. After saying goodbye to our neighbors and families, we headed for New York City to board the ship that would carry us across the Atlantic. Our little boy Arty was just three months old when we reported to the ship's captain and boarded the USS *General Rose*. I had no idea it was a troop ship, a relic from World War II. We were packed in a large room with other families and assigned a section with bunk beds and small cots. We settled into our tiny area, with barely enough room to walk around the cots that served as our beds and the small crib for Arty.

As soon as the ship reached the open sea, I began getting seasick. We were on the water for eleven days, and I was sick the entire time. I wanted to die! I did not have the strength to feed or even take care of Arty. Luckily, one of the ladies who bunked near me took over feeding him and changing his diapers. She often spent time holding him when Art was busy. I did not move off my cot because I felt so dizzy, and the room spun the moment I stood up.

After having been at sea for about five days, Art received a telegram notifying him that his assignment had been changed. He was now assigned to Udine, Italy, instead of Africa. Quite by chance, the lady, Ruth, who was taking care of Arty on the ship, and her husband were also being assigned to Udine. I felt a great sense of relief, knowing we would be traveling with people we already knew. Months later, I wondered whether this unbelievable set of circumstances had been orchestrated by my ever-present spiritual guardian, since it was an answer to my nightly prayers for protection and help.

Midway to Italy, our ship docked in French Morocco, Africa, where Art had originally been assigned. We were escorted off the ship for a few hours while the people assigned to Morocco disembarked. What a relief it was to stand on dry land! Within minutes, I was no longer sick.

We were taken to a bazaar and allowed to shop. This was like being in another world. I was spellbound to see the Arabs in their turbans and flowing robes. The women followed behind the men, covered from head to toe. Their long robes reminded me of the clothes worn by people in biblical times. The only part of their body showing was their eyes, seen through a heavy veil. I wondered how they could breathe in the oppressive heat. I suppose we looked just as odd to them in our western clothes. We women had been warned to wear only long-sleeve garments, so we would not offend the people. Morocco was an interesting place, but I was very glad we would not be stationed there for three years.

The whistle blew, and we were escorted back to the ship. As soon as we were in the open sea, I became seasick again. When we finally arrived in Naples, Italy, a few days later, I kissed the ground, vowing to never set foot on another ship again.

There were four other couples assigned to Udine, Italy, who joined us. As a group, we boarded a train for the long ride to Udine. Each family was escorted to a very comfortable private compartment on the train.

Arriving in Udine the next day, I felt rested and in good spirits. It was a good thing because while Art was being processed, he was sent to the Base Commander. He was told his assignment had been changed once again! His new assignment was to Aviano Air Force Base, which was a two-hour drive south of where we were, near a town called Pordenone, Italy. We sat in an outer office and waited for several hours while the paperwork for our transportation to Aviano was approved and finalized.

I knew that being in the military would have some drawbacks, but this was getting to be ridiculous. Aviano was going to be our home for the next three years, and as a military wife, I realized I would have to learn to adjust.

It was not easy for me to accept changes, but I'm sure my spiritual guardian knew I needed these experiences in order to learn patience.

Our military driver was a young airman who drove in from Aviano to pick us up. After we got settled into the car, the driver informed us that because Art's orders had been changed several times, there was no available housing ready for us near the base. Therefore, he had to arrange for us to stay in a hotel that was fairly close to Aviano in a town called Sacile, explaining that it was the best accommodations he could find under such short notice.

We finally pulled up in front of the hotel in the center of Sacile. I don't think the town had even eight hundred residents. Being a typical small Italian village, all the people knew each other. Actually, they were like one big family. You can imagine the excitement when we got out of the car. Because the word had spread like wildfire, nearly all the residents had come to see the Americans who would be living in their hotel. They were curious to see what an American family looked like. When Linda, eight, and Debbie, five, emerged from the car, the women smiled approvingly from ear to ear exclaiming, "Ahh, bambini!"

The men chatted in excited tones among themselves, and when I stepped out with a baby in my arms, a sound of lingering "Ahh" filled the air. I discovered that Italian people love children, and our family became a big hit. To accommodate our large family, we were given the biggest room in the hotel, which included extra beds for the children and a crib for the baby.

It took a while for us to rearrange the room and get settled. After giving Arty his last bottle of milk, I discovered there was no refrigeration in the hotel. We would have to buy an ice chest to keep his milk and baby food from spoiling. It was late, so it would have to wait until the next day for Art to find transportation to the base exchange in Aviano.

As Americans, we represented the country the Italian people knew had helped them get rid of the Nazis, and the village regarded us as special guests. As United States representatives, we knew we would have to act with dignity. We had been briefed on the importance of dressing with long sleeves when entering churches and not wearing shorts in public out of respect for their local customs.

Being in a foreign country, I feared I would have much to learn on a daily basis. What saved us months of errors was my having been raised in a French family. I immediately saw that the languages were very similar. In fact, within days, I found that many words were enough alike that by saying them in French, I would often be understood.

The immediate problem facing us was the need to buy a large piece of ice every day. On our second day, we met a young boy who could not have been more than eight years old and was a relative of the hotel owner. He agreed to bring us the ice we needed early each morning, and I offered to pay him 500 lira each day. I thought that was a fair price, since at the time, it amounted to 50 cents in American money.

After a week of this arrangement, the manager complained to me, saying I was giving the boy too much money. The average income was around 1,000 lira per week for a workingman! He said some of the men were definitely unhappy to learn the boy was making more money than they were. We had so much to learn. My biggest challenge was to learn Italian in a short period so we could communicate with everyone we had to deal with.

Thank goodness, I spoke French, but even that did not always help. We had been living in Sacile for about a month when Debbie's birthday was approaching. I wanted to order a special birthday cake to be served at our evening meal on the night of her birthday, so in my best mixed French and Italian, I asked for a *gateau*, which is French for cake. The waiter was not sure if he understood correctly, so he left and came back with the manager. The manager, wanting to be sure, asked if I was certain I wanted a *gatto* for my daughter.

"Yes, of course," I said. "I want a cake with frosting for my daughter Debbie's birthday," I repeated.

"Signora," he responded, "Are you aware that *gatto* means cat in Italian?"

Little did I know that cat was a favorite dish during the war, when food had been scarce! We all enjoyed a good laugh that night over my fractured Italian.

That conversation convinced me I would have to learn to speak Italian as soon as possible. After that, I began to constantly ask what a word meant when I spoke to anyone and how it compared with the French word

I used. As the days followed into weeks, I increased my Italian vocabulary, and within three months, I could speak Italian fairly well. I was even able to read some Italian articles. Having had a background in French made it easier to learn Italian in a shorter period. The people were impressed and extremely grateful that I took the time to learn their language. Later on, it opened many doors for me.

Living in a hotel room was less than ideal. As a matter of fact, it was downright uncomfortable and restricting. I had to take the children out for walks every day in order to get them some fresh air and sunshine. The humidity was unbearable and made the room chilly and damp. The odor of mold was everywhere. Arty began wheezing when he crawled on the floor, and at times, he had trouble breathing. It was the first signs of oncoming asthma.

For three long months, we lived in the crowded rooms the hotel had provided. Finally, after much searching, Art located a newly built house in Pordenone that was for rent. Pordenone was a fairly large town close to the base but still quite a distant commute. We learned that the majority of American families who were stationed at Aviano lived in Pordenone. We desperately wanted to get out of the hotel because it was affecting Arty's health.

The house we rented was located on a corner lot on a quiet street named Via Mamelli. Shops nearby provided daily necessities such as a bakery, produce market, and meat market. Our villa was a single story built in the Mediterranean style with white stucco walls and a red clay tile roof. We loved its interior, with black marble floors throughout, except for the three bedrooms that had hardwood floors. The grounds were surrounded with a black wrought iron fence cemented onto a three-feet-tall stone wall, giving us complete privacy. At the entrance was an electric gate that could be opened only by pressing a buzzer from inside the house. A great security feature.

Our biggest surprise was learning that Italian homes came with bare walls. There were no light fixtures anywhere in the house, no built-in closets in any of the rooms, and no cabinets in the kitchen or bathroom. The only thing in the kitchen was a sink that protruded from the wall. Luckily, our household goods had been shipped and would include our refrigerator/

freezer and washing machine, but we would have to buy cabinets for the kitchen and armoires for each bedroom for our clothes. Another necessity we needed were Italian transformers for each appliance and electrical outlets.

Once the light fixtures were installed in the ceilings, we were able to move in. When winter arrived, we needed to get sterno heaters for each room because there was no central heat in the house. All these extras were a big expense, as well as a nuisance. Thank God, we had sold our house in the states before we left because that gave us some cash in reserve. This expensive move was a drain on our finances. Some other American families were not as fortunate and had to go without necessities that we took for granted back home. It seemed like every day presented new challenges.

To add to the frustration, getting workers to show up when they said they would created countless days of wasted time while we waited for them. The laborers we encountered were always friendly, with a ready smile masking their indifference. Very few were dependable, and getting them to complete a job once started took weeks, oftentimes months, because of the incessant delays.

Another problem was getting a telephone for the house. In order to have a phone, we had to pay the city to have a telephone pole installed close by. Getting it installed took months of negotiations and constant haggling over changes. To make matters worse because Art's orders had been changed so many times, it took even longer for our household goods and furniture to be delivered.

We had barely settled into the house with the bare minimum of furnishings when Art came home with a guest for dinner one night after work. Our guest was a new arrival on the base, a Lieutenant named James. His wife Ann planned to join him soon but was having difficulty getting her passport. Without a phone, Art had not been able to call to warn me, and to make matters worse, our refrigerator had not arrived yet. We were still using an ice chest for all the perishables. The only thing I had on hand was Spam, eggs, and bread.

I fed the children first because we did not have enough room for all of us to eat at the same time. I sent them outside to play while I prepared dinner for Art, James, and me. I fried the Spam and eggs and fixed a mound of toast, wanting to at least have a filling meal. I placed an embroidered tablecloth over the card table, and we sat on wooden crates, ready to enjoy the meal. It would have been a successful meal had James not salted his eggs. When he started to put salt on them, the lid fell off the shaker and a mound of salt fell on them. I jumped up to begin cleaning the mess, making apologies, but James put me at ease by laughing hysterically. He told me not to worry, and the three of us began laughing, making the evening end in a pleasant way. A few months later, when Ann arrived, we had much to laugh about. I did not realize it at the time, but that was the first of many pleasant evenings we shared. Eventually, Ann and James became our closest friends.

After the telephone pole was installed, life was more tolerable, even quite pleasant. The next blessing was the arrival of our household goods. It was hard to believe that we had been in Italy seven months. Unpacking became a nightmare, however, because we did not have enough closet space for many of our things. We had to store some in the basement. Thankfully, the refrigerator arrived without a scratch, and our much-needed washing machine was in perfect condition. At last, we could begin living in comfort.

The following year continued to produce more challenges. Over the course of the year, I hired and fired eight maids for various reasons. Then, finally, I hired a girl from Yugoslavia who spoke fluent Italian. Her name was Marisa. She was looking for a permanent home and did not mind having to share a bedroom with Linda and Debbie. I asked her to move in with us on a two-week trial basis. I found she was very clean about her person, and she kept the house spotless. After only one week, I could see that the children preferred her company to mine and asked her to stay permanently. Within a short time, she took on the role of big sister to Linda and became the perfect nanny for Debbie and Arty. Not only was Marisa a great housekeeper, I was now free to leave the children in her care any time of day or night without worrying. Marisa became like another member of our family, and we took her everywhere we traveled.

Having Marisa live with us was the best thing that could have happened to me. Since she spoke Italian, I began to learn the language even faster. Within two months, Linda and Debbie spoke Italian as if it were their natural language. I knew I was fortunate in having found Marisa because, not only was she a caring person, she was an invaluable assistant. I could paint again and take part in the many activities that the Officers' Wives Group held weekly on the base. Marisa's only request was to have Sundays off. She even agreed to work on Sunday if it involved a special event we needed to attend.

As the days progressed, Arty's asthma symptoms worsened. I took him to the base hospital numerous times for wheezing and constant congestion, but the doctor on duty told me it was a cold and dismissed us. When Arty came down with severe diarrhea, I took him to see the doctor again. The doctor who examined him kept saying it was nothing, that Arty would outgrow the problem in time. As the diarrhea persisted, I took him back to the base several more times. The last time, a young doctor suggested that I take Arty off milk for a few days and give him only water to drink in order to clean his system. He was confident it would stop the diarrhea. That same night, when I went into Arty's room to check on him, my intuition told me something was terribly wrong.

I entered his room quietly, not wanting to wake him in case he was asleep. As I approached the crib, I saw that Arty's lips were blue and his eyes were not focusing. I screamed for Marisa to come quickly. She rushed into the room, and I asked her to call an Italian doctor right away because I had the sinking feeling that Arty was near death. "Tell him the baby is turning blue, and he has had diarrhea for several days." I hurried to dress myself while waiting for the doctor.

The doctor arrived in less than five minutes and felt the top of Arty's head. With a grim look on his face, he announced, "This baby is dehydrated and must be rushed to the hospital immediately. I hope it's not too late."

I bundled Arty in a blanket and left with the doctor in his car while Art followed in ours.

I was reminded that, had we not had Marisa, I don't know what I would have done. I certainly would not have known an Italian doctor to call or even known how to locate one in the phone book. My crash course in Italian made it possible for me to communicate with Marisa and the doctor. I was reminded that my spiritual guardian was watching over me and was sending the help I needed. Divine guidance was instrumental in saving my son's life.

I felt comfortable leaving Marisa to care for Linda and Debbie until we returned. Her presence made it possible for Art to stay with me in the hospital for as long as he needed. On the way to the hospital, I prayed, asking God to please save our little boy. I thanked him repeatedly for the help he had already sent me.

As soon as we arrived, the Italian doctor ran into the hospital with the baby in his arms and headed straight for the emergency room. Three other doctors were waiting for him, and they instantly began preparing Arty for the procedures they needed to perform. Arty was in a semiconscious state when a nurse came in with a huge syringe. She inserted it in his stomach and began giving him the forced fluids he desperately needed.

I looked up and saw three nuns enter the room. They immediately surrounded the bed and fell on their knees. In unison, they began praying in Italian. I dropped to my knees and began praying silently with them. This went on for most of the night. When Art saw there was nothing further he could do to be of any help, he went home.

As dawn approached, I was taken to a room and told to get some sleep. In the early hours of the new day, a nurse brought Arty to my room and put the sleeping baby in the crib next to my bed. The doctor came by and said the situation was now in God's hands. By late morning, the doctor who had taken me to the hospital came in to see me. He told me he felt certain that Arty was allergic to milk and said they would try him on solid foods while he was in the hospital. The nurses began feeding Arty mashed potatoes, mashed carrots, and soy milk to see how he would tolerate them. They also gave him a type of chocolate pudding made by Nestles to stop the diarrhea. It worked like magic, and within a few hours, the diarrhea began to subside. I was told to continue giving it to him daily until he was no longer having loose stools.

The second day that I was in the hospital, the American doctor I had been seeing on the base came by to see me. Art had kept him informed of what had happened and how close our son had come to dying. As soon as he walked into the room, he began apologizing, saying he regretted that he was the cause of the dire circumstances we now faced. He then informed me that he was a new doctor and not a pediatrician. I was not happy to see him and told him I did not want him to be involved with Arty's care anymore.

Before leaving, he arranged for Arty and me to be flown by emergency air evacuation to the American hospital in Wiesbaden, Germany, as soon as Arty was discharged from the Italian hospital.

Nine days later, we boarded a plane and were flown to Germany. When we arrived at the military hospital, Arty was taken from me. I was told I had to leave him and that arrangements had been made for me to be lodged in a hotel across the street. I spent every day with Arty and was able to hold him and allowed to observe what the nurses did. After two weeks of tests to determine what his problem was, I was told that Arty would have to stay in the hospital for at least three months to determine an accurate diagnosis. After two weeks in Germany, I had to leave my precious baby behind and fly back to Italy. It was a terrible experience that made me feel helpless. I was consoled by the fact that he would be getting excellent care with nurses who would hold him often.

Three months later, we were notified that Arty was well enough to come home. The exhaustive tests showed that the Italian doctor had been right. Arty was allergic to milk, as well as to several other foods. He was also allergic to his own bacteria, dust, animal fur, and dozens of tree pollens. As soon as the arrangements were made, Art and I flew to Wiesbaden. When we walked into Arty's room, Art picked him up, and the familiar hand on Art's cheek confirmed that Arty had regained his health and remembered his daddy. Time has an uncanny way of healing, and before long, our household was back to its happy way of life, though we did spoil Arty shamelessly!

* * *

Art began playing golf once a week, and once a year, he participated in a golf tournament held in a different city in Europe. That particular year the tournament was held at the Lido, next to Venice on the Grand Canal. Being close to Aviano, the wives were invited, and Art insisted that I join him. Having Marisa made it possible for me to go. The drive from Aviano to Venice took several hours. We had to travel through Vicenza and Verona, where we stopped for lunch along the way. As soon as we arrived in Venice, we parked our car and were told we would have to take a *vaporetto* (a canal boat) to travel on the Grand Canal to get to the Island of Lido.

Our accommodations were in a five-star hotel. During the four-day golf tournament, the women stayed busy playing bridge, swimming in the gorgeous pool, going shopping, and relaxing in the lovely surroundings while Italian waiters catered to our every wish. What an incredible experience that was!

For Linda's ninth birthday, we promised to buy her a piano. One of the American families was moving back to the states and offered to sell us their upright at a good price. Even though it was secondhand, it was in very good condition and had great tonal quality. Linda loved music and had talked about wanting to learn to play the piano often, so we knew she was serious. We spent a week looking for a piano teacher, and an American friend introduced us to Signora Angela Pavan, an accomplished piano teacher who had taught piano for over twenty years. She agreed to come to our house once a week to give Linda her one-hour lesson.

Hardly anyone in Italy had a car in 1957, but nearly everybody had a bicycle. I was impressed the first time Signora Pavan came to our house on her bicycle because it was a thirty-minute ride from her house. She was about ten years older than I was, in her early forties, quite attractive, and very trim. She had a knack for making me feel as if I had known her all my life. After only two weeks, we established a close friendship, and she told me to call her Angela. Before long, we developed a routine where she would stay for a cup of tea or coffee after Linda's piano lesson.

We both loved to talk, and I especially enjoyed listening to the stories she told about her life during the occupation and the terrible conditions the Italian people lived through during the war. Our visits gave me the opportunity to practice speaking Italian, speeding up my learning of the language even faster.

Angela told me about the harsh times she and her family had to endure during the Nazi occupation. The only reason her family had managed to survive with the meager rations they were allowed was because of her giving piano lessons in rural areas. She did not ask for money; instead, she exchanged piano lessons for a pound of butter or a loaf of bread. Other parents paid her with potatoes or vegetables that were in season. Depending on the time of year, she sometimes received eggs, or occasionally, a chicken. Pieces of meat from a recently butchered pig or cow were always a blessing because there was little food to be found in the stores. Milk was scarce and became a favorite exchange. She didn't mind having to bring it home in a pail slung over her bicycle handlebars—it kept her family alive and healthy.

She had learned through experience to always be alert. If she heard the faintest sound of an approaching vehicle, she quickly ran and hid herself and her bicycle in the bushes by the side of the road. It was well known that some German soldiers would stop girls at will and rape them, then abandon them like trash, as if nothing had happened. Every time she went out, she had to be on her guard. She lived in constant fear for her own safety.

Her husband had been a teacher before the war and was highly respected in the community. Unfortunately, he was badly wounded during the early part of the war and was now doing odd jobs for the few people who could afford to pay him. Having three children made it necessary for Angela to provide for the family, a daunting task in those perilous times. Hearing about her unusual experiences during World War II was fascinating. Unbelievably, the war had ended just twelve years before we met.

14

BECOMING AN ARTIST

While Linda had her piano lessons, I would set up my easel in the kitchen and paint. Being a beginner painter, I only copied pictures from magazines or other sources, working mainly with oil paints. I had a natural sense of color and concentrated on capturing detail; therefore, my work was photographic, with an occasional spurt of originality.

One afternoon when Angela finished the piano lesson, she came into the kitchen and was surprised to see me painting. They had stopped early that day, and I did not have time to put my materials away. I did not want her to see my work because, with my limited instruction, I felt self-conscious about having anyone see what I painted. She expressed surprise when she saw the landscape on the easel and exclaimed, "Signora, you do very nice work. Evidently, you have a natural talent. I can see that with lessons you could develop into a great artist. My husband takes lessons from Italy's most noted watercolor artist. His name is Professor Pio Rossi. He has been representing Italy for many years in the Biennale in Venice. He is a retired professor of art from the University of Padua and lives near us. Would you be interested in taking lessons with him? I'm sure my husband could arrange a meeting with him if you are interested."

My first reaction was, "I'm not sure he would want to teach a beginner."

"Leave it to me," Angela said. "I will have my husband speak to him. I'm sure he will want to meet you."

The following week, when she came for Linda's piano lesson, she was breathless with excitement and rushed to tell me what Professor Rossi had said. At first, he was reluctant to take on a female student because he believed women were not serious enough to be artists. He did not want to waste his time teaching a woman who would regard art as strictly a pastime or hobby. Angela's husband had to convince him I was serious, that I was different and my work showed great promise. Professor Rossi finally agreed to meet with me, mainly out of curiosity.

He told Mr. Pavan I was to come to his studio the following Wednesday at nine o'clock in the morning and to bring all of the paintings I had done up to that point so he could evaluate my work. He wanted to see for himself if I was worthy of the many hours he would have to spend with me.

In preparing for my appointment, I went through my portfolio and sorted out all the works I had done. Some were pencil drawings I had done in my early childhood, several were landscapes I had completed in oils on my own, and one was of Batista, with his hands tied behind his back just before he was executed by Fidel Castro. I had seen the picture in an American newspaper the day after it had taken place, and the look on Batista's face had moved me. I felt confident that I had captured the expression of fear recorded when one is about to die.

The day of our meeting, I was in a state of anxiety and almost ready to say forget it and not show up. But Art recognized the symptoms and talked me into going. He reminded me of how much I loved to paint and told me this might be the golden opportunity I needed to pursue my dream of becoming an artist.

I told him I was afraid of being ridiculed, and knowing that Professor Rossi did not think highly of women artists made me feel inferior. My stomach was in knots, but in his gentle way, Art put me at ease. "At least meet the man. If it doesn't work out, you will at least know that you tried."

I sat quietly for a few minutes and waited for my source of guidance to intuitively speak to me. Soon the nervous tension began to subside, and I gained the courage to leave. My intuition told me that my future as an artist depended on this interview.

The drive to the professor's house only took five minutes, and I arrived at the appointed time. When Professor Rossi greeted me, I was surprised to see that he was rather short. Because we were close in height, I felt more at ease and less intimidated. His hair was mostly gray, very curly, quite long, and rather scraggly. It reminded me of the way Albert Einstein wore his hair. What unnerved me, though, was the scowl on his face and his penetrating eyes. I swallowed hard to stay calm.

Suddenly, I recalled having done this before. I was reliving a previous experience. A distinct feeling that we had known each other a long time ago and had lost touch with each other crept into my mind. This calmed me considerably.

Professor Rossi broke the spell by asking to see my work. I reached into the trunk of the car and pulled out one painting at a time. Standing next to the car with all my paintings propped up against the side was not my idea of a fair evaluation. It made me feel like an intruder trying to sell some contraband. After fifteen minutes of the professor's intense scrutiny, I saw that he was beginning to loosen up. His expression indicated that he was impressed with what he saw.

Professor Rossi began critiquing one piece at a time, exclaiming how surprised he was at the quality of my work. He was especially pleased with the rendition of Batista and added that the other works showed promise. He hesitantly agreed to take me on as a student on a three-month trial basis. His orders were for me to come to his studio three days a week at nine o'clock in the morning, and cautioned me to never be late. If I were, he added, that will put an end to our association.

"If you want to be a serious artist, you must dedicate yourself to those three days per week. I will expect you to paint at home nearly every day, and I want you to bring what you've done for me to critique when you come for your next lesson. Those are my terms. If you agree, we can start next Monday."

Luckily, Angela had come along to see how the interview went. I needed her to translate what the professor said, and the three of us lingered and continued to talk for a while. Then the professor extended his hand, and we sealed the agreement with a handshake.

My heart pounded with excitement as I sat in my car. I couldn't wait to get home to tell Art. When he heard that Professor Rossi had accepted me as a student on a three-month trial basis, he grinned and hugged me.

He said he knew all along that my enthusiasm would captivate Professor Rossi. I was well aware that becoming his first female student-apprentice was the opportunity of a lifetime, especially knowing that Professor Rossi was Italy's most noted watercolor artist. Once again, I knew my spiritual guardian was carefully leading me to my life's destiny.

After my first week of lessons, the professor became a different person toward me. Seeing my enthusiasm and knowing that my goal was to become a great artist infused him with a renewed interest in painting. He said, being in his sixties, it made him feel young again.

The excitement I felt when I went to my painting lessons every week was exhilarating, and the professor was always happy to see me walk in the door. The profound liking we developed for each other increased as the weeks went by. I truly admired his immense talent and the freedom he expressed in his work. My goal was to become as good as he was some day.

My first lessons concentrated on copying sketches, using only a pencil. Professor Rossi stressed that he wanted to train my eyes to see the different shades of light and dark. The most important lesson in bringing life to any object was the shadows against the opposing light. One morning during the lesson, he cautioned me by saying, "Don't be in a hurry to use color. That will follow later on because it serves mainly to enhance a painting. You must first study to capture the right intensity of shadows. This is the crucial element that gives the human body and all objects form."

I began to see what he meant after we spent two months on those exercises.

A month later, I graduated from doing basic sketches and was allowed to work with pastels. This time I worked with only brown chalk to capture the shadows and highlights, and much later, I worked with charcoal sticks. Finally, he had me do sketches using pen and ink. When I became proficient with that medium, I was allowed to add watercolor washes to some of my pen-and-ink sketches. After six months of this intense training, he announced that I was ready to tackle landscapes, using oil paints.

When the weather was warm and the sun was creating shadows, I drove us to one of his favorite spots, and he taught me to paint *al fresco*. I set up my easel, and the professor set his up a short distance away. His instructions included looking through a small hole cut out of a piece of paper so I could focus on a small section of a landscape.

This small view helped me decide what part of the scene I wanted to paint. It always surprised me that we could view the same landscape yet end up with entirely different paintings.

We tried to paint outdoors as much as possible, and Professor Rossi patiently explained what to look for while I painted, often repeating that every tree is unique because the bark on each one is a different color and must be painted by following the direction of the bark. At first, I was inclined to paint everything in detail, but he taught me the importance of painting the essence of the subject, not counting every leaf and painting it precisely. I became more free and spontaneous, making the painting an original interpretation of what I saw.

Six months later, he felt I was ready to learn to use watercolors. He warned me that watercolor painting is totally different from oil painting and requires a great deal of patience. He emphasized that watercolor is not an easy medium to work with. Overworking the wet paint makes the colors turn muddy. He was right. It took a long time and many discarded attempts before I came up with a decent watercolor. Going from oil to watercolor paints was extremely difficult because they are applied differently. Oils go from dark to light. In a watercolor, on the other hand, you must determine where the light areas will be first, and then work towards achieving the medium and dark tones. After having studied for one year, I still felt like a beginner because watercolor painting was so different.

Many days, my lack of expertise in both mediums frustrated me. It was like a double-edged sword. I looked forward to the challenge, yet I feared my fumbling attempts. There were many fun days as well. Some of the most memorable were the days when we went to the hardware store to buy our art supplies. In 1957, oil paints were sold in powder form and were only available at the hardware store. They were kept in wooden bins similar to nail bins. We ordered a small amount of the color we wanted, such as cobalt blue, zinc white, yellow ochre, terra verde (green earth, his favorite color), or Venetian red. The attendant wrapped them in little packages, using white butcher paper. We also bought turpentine, linseed oil, and Damar varnish, bringing our own bottles for the clerk to fill.

When we returned to the studio, Professor Rossi showed me how to make the perfect mixture with each color. To conserve the paints, we never mixed more than what we could use that day. We arranged the colors for the day on the edge of a ceramic plate, making it our palette. At the end of the lesson, whatever paint was left on the plate we submerged in a pan of water and placed the plate on top of a black wrought iron stand. The paint stayed wet overnight and often for several days. At the start of my next lesson, I took the plate out of the water and transferred the oil paints onto a dry plate. The submerged paint was kept just as fresh as before.

During the winter months, the studio was extremely cold when I arrived. I had to wait for Professor Rossi to make a fire in the small clay stove in the far corner of the room. It took such a long time for the room to warm up that I had to keep my gloves, fur-lined boots, and heavy coat on to stay warm. After an hour, it was warm enough to remove my gloves and coat. Painting in the winter months was difficult because my hands stayed cold and my fingers would not do what I tried to accomplish. This never diminished my enthusiasm, in fact, those experiences only added to making my training noteworthy, special, and memorable.

When I completed my first year, I saw a definite improvement in my work. Professor Rossi was proud of his new female student, and he often told me how much he enjoyed our sessions. He said I had brought him a new zest for life, and he even began painting with more enthusiasm. His watercolors reflected the excitement he felt as they became more unusual, with brighter colors.

During this period, he was featured in many successful one-man shows. His work had always been in great demand and was now sold out before the end of each exhibit.

As I entered my second year as his apprentice, Professor Rossi felt I was ready for an art show. He was instrumental in making all the arrangements for a three-person show that included two other American women students, Millie and Betty, whom he had recently accepted and taught on different days. It was to be held in three months time in the Albergo Moderno Hotel located in downtown Pordenone. The other students and I began painting feverishly to assemble our best works.

The exhibit created an interest never witnessed in that small town before. The fact that we were American female artists added to the curiosity. My being an apprentice to Professor Rossi made the event even more intriguing. The exhibit was announced on the Italian radio every day for several weeks prior to the show. The local newspaper promoted it like a celebrity event, and it was even featured in *Stars and Stripes*, the military newspaper.

The night of the opening, many people sent flowers, but the most beautiful bouquet was a dozen red roses from Art. The large ballroom was packed to capacity with enthusiastic patrons. Art was at my side the entire time, beaming with pride. I told him more than once that his encouragement had made the event possible.

After the show, I was pleased that nearly all twenty-five paintings I had on display were sold. This was the first showing of American female artists in the area. I believe it started people wanting to accept women as serious painters. The Italian people were especially complimentary, as was the mayor of Pordenone and the Italian military personnel who came to the show.

Signora Pavan and her husband acted like parents who had come to witness the success and accomplishment of their child. I felt deeply indebted to Angela. It was through her insistence that I meet Professor Rossi, who brought me to this new status as a recognized artist. He now regarded me as an accomplished artist and began treating me as an equal. The highlight of the evening was when he bowed to me to show his respect and whispered, "Lucille, you have the soul of an artist."

He continued by telling everyone he had seen it in me the first day we met and that it was the reason he had accepted me as his student. That was by far the greatest compliment he could have paid me. I was so proud to hear those special words coming from him.

My first art show was an unforgettable experience. It made me realize I was entering a lifetime career as an artist, and this was just the beginning. My dream was being fulfilled, as if by divine intervention. I was aware that I needed many more years of study in order to advance in my chosen career, especially if I wanted to achieve the professional quality in my work that my instructor's paintings had.

Being a full-time mother and a dedicated student was very demanding, and I must admit, difficult at times. Having Marisa to look after the children made my pursuit of an art career possible. I could not have accomplished it without her help. Her coming into my life had been a godsend. I marveled at how God had instilled in me a love for art since childhood and how He had brought me to the other side of the world. In helping my daughter explore her love for music, the door had opened for me to study my passion with a famous artist.

I became another person when I entered the studio. I immersed myself in my work and tapped into my sixth sense. My concentration was so deep that I could not even hear. If someone spoke, I would not hear them. Often, I would notice that I was painting unconsciously, as if someone else were doing the work. Many times, I was surprised to see what I had accomplished during this wonderful state.

Professor Rossi introduced me to many painting techniques, but my favorite emerged as pen-and-ink sketches with watercolor washes. I created unusual works using that method. We continued to go on our paint-outs every week, and we would bring a stack of precut wooden boards already primed to paint on. Using oil paints for these quick paintings, the professor taught me to spend no more than fifteen minutes to capture just the impression of what I saw. When we returned to the studio later on, these became our subjects for larger canvases. This taught me to paint fast. I could paint a beautiful landscape in less than twenty minutes. The more spontaneously I worked, the better it would be. Professor Rossi became very complimentary of my work, and one day he surprised me by saying, "The master eventually learns from the student."

15

EUROPEAN ADVENTURES

By now, Art and I had been socializing with our friends every Friday night at the Officer's Club. We still felt like newlyweds and enjoyed every moment we spent together. Living in Italy had turned out to be one of the best experiences of my life.

Every year, when Art had his vacation, we spent it visiting different European countries. We brought the children along, as well as Marisa. For the first time in her twenty-three years, Marisa was able to travel and see other parts of Europe. Having her with us gave Art and me the freedom to go out at night while she stayed with the children. One of our first trips was to Munich, Germany. Driving through the Brenner Pass, we marveled at the lovely winter scenes and gorgeous countryside. Linda and Debbie loved the excitement. We stayed in Cortina the first night of the trip. After dinner, we all went ice skating as a group and laughed hysterically as we propped each other up and fell in heaps every now and then.

The following year, we went to Paris. Having to travel through several countries gave us the opportunity to see many cities in Italy and Germany. We were awestruck by the olive groves and the never-ending vineyards covering the hillsides. Art made reservations at the Hotel Napoleon in Paris, which overlooked the L'Arc de Triomphe. It was only a block and a half from our hotel. After we checked in, we were able to see it clearly from our balcony. Before we were assigned our rooms, Art was told that there had been a mistake in our reservation and the hotel was totally booked. They did not have any rooms large enough to accommodate our family of six. The manager was called to figure out what arrangements could be made to accommodate us. When the manager learned about the reservation error, he was appalled. He graciously apologized to Art and added that the only thing he could do was assign us to the presidential suite. Since it was their mistake, he would have us moved into the suite for the same price Art had been quoted when he made the reservation. I could not believe the unexpected change of plans. Being escorted to the presidential suite for our week's stay became the thrill of a lifetime. Talk about serendipity—or was it divine intervention once again?

Our luggage was immediately brought up with great fanfare and countless apologies. As we entered, seeing the luxury of the rooms was beyond my wildest expectations. The antique furniture in every room was from the Napoleon period. There were gold accents everywhere. I could almost visualize Napoleon sitting on the brocade-covered reclining lounge chair.

Before too much time had elapsed, our doorbell rang. Art answered it to find a chambermaid with towels. A short time later, the doorbell rang again. This time, it was a porter asking if we wanted our shoes shined. The third time our bell rang, it was a waiter wanting to know what we desired to eat. It did not take long to discover that Arty had climbed up on a chair and was pushing the many buttons on the wall. Before long, every servant had been summoned and knocked at our door. Luckily, I spoke French and was able to make excuses for our little boy. This only added to our enjoyment, and we laughed about it for years.

The next day, we took the children to see the Eiffel Tower. Debbie could not pronounce it, so she called it the "elephant tire" whenever she talked about it. Another day, we took everyone for a horse and buggy ride around the Champs-Elysées. Later in the day, Art and I toured the Louvre, leaving Marisa with the children at the hotel. It was wonderful to be able to admire the Mona Lisa painting close up. At that time, it was displayed on the wall without any type of protection, like all the other famous paintings. The statue of the Winged Victory of Samothrace featured at the top of the stairs was magnificent. Even without a head, it took my breath away. I could not envision how the artist could capture the folds of cloth while working with marble. I was inspired and greatly impressed viewing the paintings of the French Impressionists. Many were my favorite painters. Seeing their work gave me goose bumps. I studied them closely and wanted to be able to capture the movement they expressed some day in my own paintings.

The following year, we went to Rome. My joy had no bounds as we visited the Trevi Fountain, the Coliseum, the Forum, Vatican City, the Sistine Chapel, and the many other cathedrals and churches. Everywhere we went was a site more beautiful than the previous. I must admit that the sculpture that impressed me most was Michaelangelo's Pietà in St. Peter's Basilica. The way he achieved the life-like proportions and detail carved out of marble seemed impossible. There were so many fountains scattered all over the city of Rome that every turn on another street revealed yet another one of exceptional design and beauty.

Living in Italy gave us the opportunity to vacation in places like Florence, Venice, Vicenza, and Verona, where Romeo serenaded Juliet. I even took pictures of the balcony where Juliet stood looking down at her Romeo. What an unexpected adventure!

Every town we visited was packed with historical sites to see. We toured the Leaning Tower in Pisa, and Livorno, with its docks and beaches. We saw firsthand how the old city of Naples had crowded streets as narrow as alleyways. There was not enough room for a car to get by. The buildings were so close together that I wondered how people were able to get around on the bicycles that appeared everywhere. Clothes were hung to dry on clotheslines that stretched across the narrow street from one building to another on the other side. They made me think of kites, flapping over our heads as we walked. No matter where we went, the endless surprises made each trip interesting and a lot of fun. Our dinners were often seven-course meals, allowing us plenty of time to enjoy new treats and local wines with each course.

We enjoyed many trips to Germany, and one of my favorite cities was Garmisch, situated high in the mountains. It is so quaint because nearly every building is painted on the outside with German scenes. Whenever we went to Garmisch, Art registered to stay at the General Patton Hotel, which was reserved for American military personnel. It is located very close to the Zugspitze, Germany's highest mountain. The excitement and sheer thrill of the journey by cable car up to the summit was like something from a James Bond movie. Once at the top, the view from the observation deck was the most incredible sight I had ever imagined. It was so high that the clouds surrounded our heads. How they were able to build the observation deck and a restaurant at such a high altitude was unbelievable.

Another place we enjoyed was Innsbruck, Austria. Our first trip was when Art played in a golf tournament. After that, we went as often as we could, just for the beauty of the scenery and to see the many interesting places surrounding the area. We especially enjoyed eating in the famous local restaurants.

Life in Europe in the late 1950s was an unforgettable experience. The people lived a simple life, rich with history, and I absorbed all this new culture like a sponge. There was so much to see and do in Europe. Three and a half years was not nearly enough time to see all the magnificent places we wanted to visit.

Our Italian neighbors became close friends, and their children were constant playmates for Linda and Debbie. Whenever they were not at home, they were at their friends' houses, having a grand time learning to play new games.

Art was in charge of personnel for the entire base, giving him many responsibilities. These included overseeing not only the needs of the military personnel but also hiring civilian employees for countless jobs, including teachers for the elementary and high schools located on the base. It was an invaluable job experience for him.

Our social life was filled with functions that took place at the Officer's Club, with mandatory dinners promoted by the base commander and his wife. During those events, the commander invited Art and me to sit at the head table so I could interpret the conversation taking place with the Italian guests. While stationed at Aviano, we had three different base commanders. None of them spoke Italian, so my services were always needed. This gave me the unimaginable opportunity to meet the Italian dignitaries who attended the events on the base.

As a family, we formed the habit of speaking only Italian at home, and nearly every day Marisa taught us new words. I also spoke Italian exclusively with Angela and Professor Rossi. During our conversations, I learned words I had not encountered before—an ideal circumstance that helped me learn colloquial expressions—lessons I could not have gotten from books. At the time, I did not realize how much they were helping me. Even the children began speaking Italian fluently because they were with Marisa most of the time. In fact, Italian was Arty's first language.

The time was drawing near for us to leave Italy. Art's assignment was coming to a close. Just thinking about it made my heart ache. I did not want to leave the wonderful life we had established, and of course, the many wonderful friends we had made. When Art's orders arrived, he was put on notice that he was to report to his new assignment within a month. Much to our surprise and delight, Art's new assignment was in Washington, D.C. He was assigned to the Pentagon in the Air Force Legislative Liaison section. The news boosted our energy, and we began packing in earnest.

We attended farewell parties given by our many friends. How I dreaded having to leave them because my intuition told me we would probably never see them again. My most agonizing thought was that the time would come to have to say goodbye to Professor Rossi, Marisa, and Angela. That would be heartbreaking. A few weeks later, when the movers were packing our household goods, Professor Rossi came to our house on his bicycle to say goodbye. He made me promise to write to him often, and after a long-lasting hug, we reluctantly parted. Seeing him leave with his shoulders slumped forward, visibly crying, made me break down. I would remember this man, my mentor, for the rest of my life. By giving me the instructions and the confidence I needed to become an accomplished artist, he truly changed my life.

Saying goodbye to Marisa was another matter. She had become such a big part of our family that it was difficult to even utter the words. Her selfless caring for all of us was remarkable. She never complained and always showered us with affection. As I hugged her for the last time, Art had to break us apart because we could not let go of each other. As hard as it was for Art and me to go through this, leaving was even harder on the children. They cried and held on to Marisa, as I had done. It was a traumatic event that they would never forget.

After getting our household packed and shipped, we got into our car and headed for Livorno, next to Pisa. Even I was happy to board a ship called the SS *Constitution* for the return trip to the United States. I had been apprehensive about setting foot on another ship, remembering my horrible experience on the troop ship in 1956. But when I learned that the SS *Constitution* was considered one of the finest luxury cruise liners of the time, I relaxed and felt confident I would enjoy the trip. We sailed out to sea, and a few hours later, I did not feel dizzy or seasick at all, much to my delight. I had a fabulous time the entire week we were on the Atlantic Ocean.

Our family was assigned to a large stateroom with its own private bath. We spent most of our time onboard enjoying the many amenities. The children preferred to stay in the playroom, watching movies and playing with the other children. Our assigned table had a private waiter for each meal, and the food choices were unbelievable. The constant activities kept us busy the entire time we were onboard. When we arrived in New York City, I was frankly sad to leave the ship because it had been such a fabulous experience.

Now that we were on dry land, I began getting excited about seeing my mother and other relatives again. I wondered how we would react to the many changes that awaited us. Linda and Debbie were especially excited about seeing their cousins, their grandmothers, and the many other relatives. Arty, on the other hand, could not fathom what the fuss was all about. He clung to me, wondering where in the world he was. When he got tired, he cried and asked for Marisa. It took him a month to get used to not having her around.

16

RETURNING TO THE U.S.

By the time we got back to the states, Art had accrued enough leave time for a two-week vacation. After getting our car in Brooklyn, New York, we headed straight for Connecticut and New Hampshire. I called my mother as soon as we got off the ship and made plans to visit my side of the family first. Everyone was looking forward to seeing the children, especially Arty, who was approaching four years old. What a change that was going to be, since he was only three months old when we left.

Mother was overjoyed when she saw us. For the first few days, everybody was captivated by Arty, who spoke broken English. He had everybody laughing when he said things like, "Ima nota gonna" for "I'm not going to."

He had never seen a plum, and after sampling one, he began asking for a "purple peach." He made up countless new words that had us hysterical for days. His little-boy antics kept us running to keep him out of trouble. He was a bundle of energy and had no concept of fear, and I had to watch him constantly because the apartments we visited were not on ground level.

Linda, nearly twelve years old, was no longer the little girl her grandmother had said goodbye to. She had become quite the young lady. Mother was taken aback when she saw signs that Linda would be wearing a bra soon and that she had grown into a real beauty with her big blue eyes and long golden blond hair.

Debbie was a delightful nearly seven-year-old and already quite the little diplomat. She happily went to everyone, as if she had been around them all her life, allowing them to lavish kisses and bear hugs on her at will. After our first day, she had captured everybody's heart. Her dark brown hair was a mass of curls, and her dark brown eyes were always sparkling. She, too, was a striking beauty.

My family reunion ended after only one week—not really enough time to make up for the many years we had been away. But it had to suffice. We still had to visit Art's parents and the other relatives in Connecticut, so we moved on.

Happily, Art's Uncle Steve owned a large beach house close to the water, and the family gathered there for our big reunion. The festivities were nonending; we gathered on the beach and played games, and the evenings were packed with parties. The family could not do enough to show us how much they had missed us. After spending a week with them, we had to leave for Washington, D.C., to establish our new home.

When we arrived in Washington, we checked into a hotel for several weeks to give us time to decide where we wanted to live. Not knowing the area, Art decided to hire a real estate agent. After looking for several weeks, we found a house outside of Washington in Springfield, Virginia. The location was perfect—close to the Pentagon, close to schools, and near many shopping areas. Another great feature was that it was only one block from the elementary school Debbie would attend and the bus stop that would take Linda to the junior high school. Although the house was pre-owned, it had been kept up like a new house. The features were quite impressive but did not lessen the shock of the $22,000 purchase price, which was a fortune in my estimation. Art had to convince me that we could afford it without going into debt for the rest of our lives. The neighborhood had a swimming pool with a clubhouse for members just a short walk from our house. This new concept had been established while we lived in Italy. It later became the norm for new developers.

The next few months were filled with a blur of activities. We had to wait for quite some time before our household goods arrived, so getting settled took more time than we expected. Once we had the house in order, we were able to enjoy our new neighbors and the fabulous neighborhood.

The constant activities did not stop me from yearning for my friends in Italy, especially my mentor, Professor Rossi. When we were sufficiently settled, I began writing to him as I had promised. The wait for his reply kept me checking the mail with the same anticipation one feels when a gift is on its way. When his letters did arrive, they restored my enthusiasm, the balm that made me feel whole again.

Each morning, after the children left for school, I took Arty to preschool and then rushed home. As soon as the household chores were done, I set up my easel and paints in the dining room. I felt an urgency to paint until midafternoon, and then I put everything away before the children came home from school. The rest of the day I devoted to taking Linda and Debbie to piano or ballet lessons, picking up Arty, and entertaining him until it was time to get the girls again.

* * *

Before two months had gone by, I entered art shows that were being promoted in the area. Later on, I joined the Northern Virginia Art League and made friends with several artists who were serious painters like me. The Art League was a busy organization with an active membership that promoted sidewalk art shows every month. I looked forward to participating in the shows, and before long, I began winning awards on a regular basis. The first time I sold one of my paintings at a sidewalk show, I could barely contain my excitement.

As a benefit for being a member of the Art League, I was invited to have a private showing of my work in the Springfield, Virginia, city hall. I had been told that those exhibits were by invitation only to local artists who had won awards and showed promise of becoming recognized. You can imagine my surprise to be featured in a one-person show for an entire month. It was my first art exhibit in the United States and was highly promoted by the local newspaper. A reporter came to my house for a personal interview that included taking pictures of some of my paintings, including a dozen shots of me standing at my easel with a painting propped on it. The article appeared the following week as a full-page spread, featuring me standing at my easel surrounded by my paintings. The headline read: woman finds herself in italy with a brush.

The exhibit made it possible for me to sell many of my paintings and gave me tremendous local exposure. The article received so much attention that I began getting phone calls to do public speaking engagements for different organizations.

One in particular was an adult education class about Italy. They contacted me because, being close to Washington, D.C., they wanted me to introduce the guest speaker from the Italian Embassy at their next meeting. I was told the audience would consist of over five hundred people in an auditorium setting. Frankly, I did not want to do it, but Art talked me into going by saying it would be a great way for me to become known and an invaluable way to advance my career. I decided to give it a try. Doubts began forming in my mind, knowing I had no experience in public speaking. I wondered if I should go through with it.

When the night arrived and I was introduced, I could feel my legs shaking as I walked to the podium. I closed my eyes for a second and said a silent prayer, asking my spiritual guardian for composure and divine guidance. Instantly, I felt a gentle breeze cross my face and shoulders. Looking ahead at the sea of faces in the audience, all I could see was a foggy blur and I began to speak. I knew my prayer had been answered because the calming feeling I felt was instantaneous. After that experience, I no longer feared talking in front of groups. It helped me overcome the shyness that had plagued me all my life.

That was the beginning of many requests for me to do speaking engagements. The requests usually were for me to talk about my life in Italy. People were interested in learning everything about the way people lived and their customs. They found what I had to say very exciting, especially because I had studied art in Italy as the apprentice of a famous artist. It definitely created interest for the artists in the audience, who wanted to hear details about my art training with Italy's most noted watercolor artist of that period.

Another invitation to speak came from the minister of our church. I had talked with him several times about my beliefs, and being interested in my early childhood experiences, he wanted me to share them with the congregation by giving a sermon at one of our Sunday morning services. When that particular Sunday arrived, the person who was supposed to give a sermon at the second service became ill and was unable to speak. As a favor to the minister, I agreed to give my sermon at both services.

As the word spread that I was an artist, many people began asking me to give art lessons at our church. When fifteen people said they were interested, I decided to teach an art class one day per week. After the first month, I decided to charge a minimal fee because too many people wanted to join the class. Since exchange of money was not allowed in our church, I suggested to the minister that I donate ten percent of my monthly fees to the church. He agreed that as a donation, it would be allowed.

After six months, the class was overflowing and I had to start a second class. When that class filled up, I had to implement a waiting list. Before long, I was teaching three classes each week and regarded as an accomplished art instructor.

Two of my students, Romayne and Betty, became my closest friends. Our passion for art was mutual, plus we definitely had a lot in common. One day the three of us decided to enroll in an art class at the Corcoran Gallery of Art in Washington, D.C. The class was held in the morning, so it did not interfere with my scheduled commitments. We studied art at the Corcoran with different instructors off and on for a while.

We took turns driving to class, and after the session, stopped for lunch and spent an extra hour visiting the many art galleries in downtown Washington, getting acquainted with the current tends. The three of us wanted to learn everything we possibly could that involved visual art. One month, the Corcoran featured an exhibit of a famous watercolor artist named Andrew Wyeth. I was overwhelmed when I saw his work and impressed that he could capture such detail using watercolors. I'm sorry to say I was not able to buy one of the paintings I fell in love with for $800. Twenty years later, his paintings were selling in the millions of dollars.

Eventually, Romayne, Betty, and I decided we were ready to advance our careers and needed to learn new techniques from individual instructors. We enrolled at the American Society of Fine Arts, also located in downtown Washington, D.C. To our delight, we learned the classes were on a day-to-day basis and hourly. We could attend whatever day we wanted, making it extremely convenient for us.

One of our instructors was an Armenian named Miran. He had moved to the U.S. from Iran sometime in the 1950s. Since my husband Art was Armenian, it helped me form a close relationship with Miran. Even though his style was totally different from mine, I was confident I could learn much from him.

The other instructor was named Tom. His style was more traditional and impressionistic. He introduced me to palette knife painting techniques using oil paints. He was extremely diversified and taught me how to paint over wax drawings, mono prints, and block prints and shared various watercolor techniques. Those classes became the highlight of my week. I learned so much, and my work improved steadily—to the point that I began winning awards in almost every show I entered. One judge even commented that my work was "visionary."

As my art career blossomed, I was still very much involved with my family and friends. I decided to end the classes at our church and began teaching exclusively in my home. Many of the students followed me, and I now taught three classes per week in my dining room.

Since our dining room was small, I could accommodate only six students at a time. They brought a sack lunch, and we stopped for lunch around noon. During lunch, we had serious discussions about art, including some important debates about the new art forms that were taking place. At the end of the lesson, I critiqued their work.

Betty, Romayne, and I continued going into D.C. to visit art galleries once a week and study the works of famous artists, a lesson in itself. I observed their brush strokes, the detail, and their perspective. I especially examined their use of color, until the use of color became my predominant strength. The thing that stood out for me was the distinct styles each artist was noted for. I began noticing the looseness each artist had perfected in their work. I made it my goal to develop a style that would define my work some day.

I began working consciously to develop a unique style, so that when someone walked into a gallery or a home, if they saw one of my paintings, they would recognize it immediately without having to look at the signature. I observed that a committed artist is never really satisfied with their work, no matter how great the work is. When you think you've arrived, you become complacent and stop growing. Every time I paint, I learn something new, leaving me surprised and amazed. I finally understood why they say that to become an artist requires many years of trial and error, but most of all patience.

* * *

While I was busy with the children and my art career, Art was enjoying his work as a Legislative Liaison officer in the Pentagon. His office dealt with a young senator from Massachusetts named John F. Kennedy, Senator Lyndon Johnson from Texas, and Speaker of the House John McCormack.

Occasionally, Art invited me to have lunch with him in the Senate dining room in the Capitol building. Those lunches were the highlight of my day. As I looked around the room and observed the senators, congressmen, and many other influential people that I would sometimes see on TV at night, I was aware of the privilege it was to be living in Washington. Never in my wildest dreams did I ever imagine that one day I would be eating in the same dining room with all those important people.

As I became more familiar with those surroundings, I requested permission to take our relatives to the Senate dining room whenever we had company. Art made the arrangements and I picked up our passes in Speaker McCormack's office. I did not abuse this privilege, since I knew how special it was to be included on this VIP list.

Frequently, I took our visitors to the National Mall area of Washington to see the monuments. If we had enough time, we'd complete the day by visiting the Smithsonian Institution, where we would spend hours yet never cover every floor because there was always too much to see and do.

I always had a terrible time remembering names; therefore, when I read that you could overcome this problem by using word association, I used that process often. For one of my planned visits to the Senate dining room, I contacted an aide to make the reservations. When we arrived, I told the person in Senator McCormick's office that I was picking up our passes. He asked who had arranged my visit, and I told him a Mr. Flagherty. He left, and five minutes later, he returned and told me to be patient—that they were trying to locate Mr. Flagherty. Ten more minutes went by, and I was told they could not find anyone with that name who worked in their offices. I quickly blurted out, "Umm, name someone in the office with an Irish name."

He quickly responded, "Well, we do have a Mr. Dougherty."

"That's it!" I exclaimed.

Oops, talk about being embarrassed!

Another name-association event that went badly happened when one of Art's coworkers named Robert was promoted to full colonel. We were invited to his promotion party, which took place in a very expensive and elegant hotel in Washington. His wife Patricia was a close friend of mine and was looking forward to the event because her art teacher was going to be there, and she wanted us to meet. She felt certain that since we had a lot in common, we might end up becoming close friends. She had tried several times before to have us meet, but it never seemed to work out. This presented the perfect opportunity.

Art and I arrived at the party and were immediately asked what we would like to drink. I asked for a martini. Within five minutes of our arrival, Patricia spotted me and came running over, giddy with excitement. She told me her art teacher had just arrived and was busy talking with another guest, but as soon as she was free, she would bring her over. More time passed, and I had a second martini. We were having such a great time mingling with our other friends that, before I knew it, I was on my third martini. Not being a drinker, I was in a very happy state when Patricia finally came running over with her art teacher in tow.

"At last, Lucille, this is my art teacher, Mrs. Gaydash."

Smiling and flushed, I blurted out, "Oh, what a wonderful name for a horse!"

I must say, Mrs. Gaydash was not amused. I tried to explain my word association, "You know, gaydash, race horse."

She would hear none of it and walked off in a huff. You can well believe I never forgot her name.

17

REVELATIONS

We had been in Virginia nearly three years when I discovered I was pregnant again. The morning sickness I was experiencing made it necessary for me to stop doing everything. Taking the girls to their ballet lessons every week was a necessity, but my other activities had to be curtailed. Eventually, I had to stop giving art lessons in my home. I found the changes hard at first, but with all the added free time, my interest in reading was renewed.

My thoughts focused on my life and how this new child would change it yet again. It became a period of searching for the meaning of my existence. I suppose it was a transformation I did not fully understand. Through times of quiet, I reflected on my childhood years and the many times my spiritual guardian had helped me. I knew this was the same source for the inspiration I was still receiving. I almost felt unworthy of the help. The creative juices that had flown into my paintings began flowing into my poetry—another form of art I absolutely loved. This was a new outlet of self-expression for me and was exciting beyond belief. Writing poems became so spontaneous that many times I did not believe I had written them. Sitting in a meditative state, words formed in my mind and I quickly wrote them down.

One day I was inspired to write a poem, and these words came easily from my heart:

God's Hand
Sometimes when I start painting,
I feel God's presence near

Guiding my hand that fumbles
To capture His breathless sphere

A dab of red, a dab of gold,
And then perhaps some blue,
His inspiration constant now
As I brush on lasting hue.

The subject comes alive at last
On canvas once so bare.
God's will has captured once again
A breadth that is so rare.

Though I'll pass on and be forgot,
These works I'll leave behind
In memory of God's hand
With heart and soul entwined.

As my pregnancy progressed, I began feeling strange. I knew something was wrong, but the doctor assured me at each visit that the baby was doing fine. In my seventh month of pregnancy, my ankles began to swell and large round blotches began appearing all over my body. I made an emergency appointment to see my doctor when more blotches began showing up. He was concerned and put me on a strict diet, plus he gave me some medication to control fluid retention.

At my next appointment several weeks later, he checked the baby's heart beat and was shocked to find there was none to be heard. He could not believe it. In my seventh month, the baby had died in my womb. The dead fetus was now poisoning my blood. I began experiencing constant labor pains, but they did not increase to the extent that the baby was dropping and allowing real labor to start. The doctor insisted I let nature take its course. Finally, after two weeks of constant labor pains, he had me come to the hospital for an evaluation with three other doctors. Each one had a different opinion. They could not agree on how to proceed. They did agree that I would die if they performed a Caesarean section because the poison would enter the bloodstream and quickly spread throughout my body. Eventually, my obstetrician went against the other doctors' opinions because he was concerned for my well-being. He decided to induce labor.

After being prepped for the procedure, I was put in a bed and taken to the front of the nurse's station so the nurses could keep a constant watch over me. This was very embarrassing because everybody who walked by would look at me. I felt like I was on display. After I'd spent three days in front of the nurses' station, still with constant labor pains, the doctor knew the inducement had not worked. I was finally moved to a private labor room, where another day went by and still nothing happened.

At this stage, I began feeling my body getting much weaker. I could not eat, and my vital signs were not good. I could tell they had given up on me. The doctors told me I had been given all the labor-inducing serum they could safely administer. My body was going into toxic shock. The next day, the doctor informed me that my condition was grave and added that the outcome was now in God's hands. As I lay in my weakened condition, I began to pray like never before. "Dear God, I don't want to die. My children need me. Please let this baby come out, and let me live."

Sometime later, the room took on that familiar foggy mist, and I was surrounded with a bright light that was almost blinding. Through the haze, I saw a figure appear at the foot of my bed. He was so tall that his head touched the ceiling. I could clearly see him and was nearly blinded by the brightness of his long white robe. His bare feet were at eye level. His hands were outstretched, like he was calling me to him. Suddenly, a wonderful feeling of peace came over me and I was no longer afraid. We began communicating with our thoughts. He told me I had much to do before I was to leave this earth, and I must search my soul to find out why I had chosen to be born. The words that I had a mission to accomplish in this lifetime stayed in my subconscious mind. He reminded me that he watched over me and would continue to do so, and then just as suddenly as he appeared, the room went dark and he vanished.

At that very moment, I felt the baby slide out of my body. I yelled for the nurses and kept yelling until one finally came. I told her the baby had just slipped out. She carefully looked and was shocked at what she saw. I asked to see the baby but the nurse said, "No, honey. You don't want to see this."

She then put a mask on my face and wheeled me into the delivery room. The ether quickly worked its blessed effect, and some time later, I woke up in a private room, with Art at my side. We hugged and cried together, both of us realizing how close I had come to dying. I was kept in the hospital for one week to make sure that all the poison was gone from my system. When I returned home, I was a different person. Often, I thought back and wondered, did I truly see that apparition, or was it a figment of my imagination? As time went on, I relived that moment and knew it was real.

The sadness Art and I felt at losing the baby brought us closer and made us aware of how precious our time was with Linda, Debbie, and Arty. As soon as I walked into our house, all three ran to me, hugged me, and wanted to be by my side constantly. We certainly had missed each other. While looking at them, I finally understood that children are a gift from God and must never be taken for granted. That, as parents, it is our duty to teach them, especially right from wrong.

I now wanted to become the best mother I could possibly be. I devoted myself to encouraging my children to strive to accomplish whatever they wanted to achieve in life. I began teaching them that anything was possible. I made certain they knew about the spiritual side we all are born with and how important it is to develop our spirit, not just our material side.

The more I thought about it, the more I accepted that I was truly visited by a divine being that day. I knew beyond any doubt that the spiritual guardian who visited me had watched over me my entire life. He made me aware that there is more to life than what we perceive as human beings with our five senses. I don't know if I was in the presence of Jesus, a guardian angel, or one of the saints. I do know that I was not dreaming. The image of that being, so tall and radiant, in a flowing white robe with outstretched hands, will always remain fixed in my mind. I no longer took life for granted. When you come that close to dying, an inner knowing of what lies beyond this life changes you.

When the time presented itself, I went to our church and visited with our pastor. When I told him about my vision, he was dumbfounded and almost jealous at what I had seen and experienced. He asked me if I would be willing to give a sermon about it sometime. As usual, I was reluctant, but after thinking it over, the ever-present voice told me this was part of the work I was expected to do. I spoke of my experiences not only in that sermon but whenever I felt the revelation would help someone.

After a period of recuperation, my home life eventually returned to normal. It was sad and difficult to give away all the new baby clothes I had received, and having to dispose of the baby items we had purchased was upsetting. I felt a void for a long time, but time has a way of making us forget. Eventually, I decided to go back to giving art lessons and began painting regularly once again.

The following January, Senator John F. Kennedy was sworn in as President of the United States, and Lyndon Johnson became Vice President. Since Art worked directly with their offices involving legislative liaison, we received an invitation to attend the inauguration. A separate invitation was included to attend one of the balls. Unfortunately, we had to decline. It would have been too costly on our limited budget, plus the logistics to attend were much too complicated. At the time, we were content to have received the invitations. That was more than enough to give us the thrill of a lifetime. The invitation and inauguration medal depicting the Kennedy and Johnson profiles became treasured keepsakes.

During this historic time, the United States was very involved with the cold war that was still raging with Russia. We were warned daily that an atomic attack was possible in the D.C. area. We were all briefed and encouraged to have a special place in the house to go to in case of an attack. After much discussion, Art and I decided to use the space under the stairs in the lower part of our tri-level house. It seemed the safest place in case of an attack. The children helped us gather what we thought we would need, in case we had to spend time in our shelter. We stocked a trunk full of provisions, medical supplies, and blankets. Twice a month we practiced our evacuation plans.

President Kennedy was deeply involved with the Bay of Pigs Invasion with Cuba and Russia. The threat of war was imminent and frightening. It kept us in a state of watchful anxiety, especially since our proximity to the White House and the Pentagon put us in the target range. We watched the evening news on television with renewed interest, always mindful and afraid of what lay ahead.

When Art received orders for his new assignment in July, we were more than ready for a change. He was especially happy to learn that he was being assigned to the personnel headquarters at Randolph Air Force Base in San Antonio, Texas.

After spending three wonderful years in the Washington, D.C., area, it was time to move once again. I wondered what new adventures awaited us. On his last day at work, Art was awarded the Commendation Medal for outstanding job performance. That award was considered a great honor. The formal presentation took place in the Capitol building, with the children and me in attendance. The year before, Art had been promoted to Major, another testament to his outstanding work.

As the days went by, Art was busy finalizing his work at the Pentagon. Part of my responsibilities involved selling the house. Fortunately, during the three years we spent in Virginia, the house had increased in value and would be a big help financially because relocating was always expensive.

As always, leaving our friends was not going to be easy, especially leaving my art buddies. But we promised to stay in touch and to write often. I still wrote to Professor Rossi several times a week and looked forward to his letters. We continued our correspondence until his death, eight years later.

Having lived on the east coast for three years made it possible for me to see my mother often, but now I had the difficult task of telling her goodbye once more. Mother had married while we were in Italy. Her husband George was extremely fond of us, and whenever they came to visit, it was almost like Christmas for the children because they always brought along a car trunk full of presents. I was grateful that the children had the opportunity to really get to know their wonderful grandparents. During our three years in Virginia, we had been fortunate to have my in-laws close by. In fact, we saw everybody quite often. Moving to Texas was going to present a big change for all of us. That was one of the drawbacks of being in the military. We had to learn to adjust to a move every three years.

18

LIVING IN TEXAS

The day we arrived in San Antonio, the temperature was 104 degrees. Our car was not air-conditioned, so it must have been at least 115 degrees inside. It was so hot that I imagined this must surely be what hell feels like. I had never experienced such extreme heat in my entire life. To make matters worse, the housing accommodations on the base were not yet available, and we had to stay in the Visiting Officers Quarters with just our luggage. Sharing small rooms with three children, especially Linda, who was a teenager of thirteen, deprived us of any privacy. It made for an unpleasant situation, to say the least.

My first impression of Randolph AFB and San Antonio was not favorable. More than once, I was sorry we had left our comfortable, beautiful house in Virginia. To pass the time, I took the children to the base library almost every day. This had always been one of their favorite pastimes, and it made the days go by faster. When we became more familiar with the base, I discovered all the amenities it had to offer. There was a movie theater, a bowling alley, and an 18-hole golf course with a clubhouse that was reputed to make the best hamburgers in the area. The Officer's Club had an Olympic-size swimming pool, as well as a children's pool. With the oppressive heat that wouldn't let up, it became one of our favorite places to hang out. I told the children we would be living on the base for a long time, so we may as well have a good time and pretend we were on a long vacation. Once our attitude changed, we began to enjoy ourselves. Before the month was out, Linda, Debbie, and Arty had formed new friendships.

I had also made friends with several women who I enjoyed being with. Our unencumbered lifestyle became quite pleasant, with no housework to do and no cooking. I relaxed and began having fun every day. After being at Randolph AFB just a short time, we learned it was known as the jewel of all the air force bases.

Art was happy with his new job, especially when he learned that being in the personnel center at Randolph was considered a plum assignment. He had a great sense of humor and joked with everyone he met. Within the first month, everyone in the office considered him a best friend.

After we moved into permanent housing, life became a whirlwind of excitement. I enrolled the children in the base elementary school, junior high, and high school. Each one was close to the house, with bus pickup practically at our front door. Within a week, I hired a wonderful woman who came once a week to clean the house. She even did the ironing—a chore I had always detested!

My days were free to pursue my art career full time once again. At the end of the summer, when school started, I devoted most of my free time to painting. I joined the local art leagues and participated in the art shows that were promoted on the base, plus several that took place in San Antonio.

I noticed that the more I painted, the more unexpected discoveries flowed. I experimented with oil paints and gesso, and found the new mediums that had been introduced to the art market in the 1960s helped me develop several unique styles. With an endless source of creative ideas, I entered nearly all the art competitions in the area. The most gratifying part was seeing my artwork sell all the time. I had to paint almost daily to keep up with the commission demands and the sales. The 1960s became extremely productive years for me.

* * *

One November day, when we had been in Texas four months, I had the strongest urge not to paint and instead to visit my next-door neighbor, June. She had invited me numerous times, but I was always too busy. Besides, I did not like to sit around making small talk and considered it a waste of my time. This particular day, I sensed a need to get out of the house, and I did not want to be alone.

I knocked on June's door. When I walked in, the radio was playing, and she left it on while we talked. After only fifteen minutes, the program stopped. The announcer came on and tearfully told the listeners that President John Kennedy had just been shot while visiting Dallas, Texas. It was November 22, 1963—a day I will never forget.

The impact of that news made me feel like I had lost a member of my own immediate family. My body began to shake. June and I hugged and sobbed uncontrollably. It took me over an hour to regain my composure and start thinking clearly. When I looked at the clock, I saw that it was time for my children to arrive home from school. I left in a daze, unable to believe what I had just heard. I'm glad I was at my neighbor's house when I heard the news because, if I had been by myself, I don't know how I would have reacted.

When the children walked in, it was evident they had been told at school because they were sad and wanted me to explain what had happened. We watched the replays of the assassination on television and the swearing in of Vice President Lyndon Baines Johnson in Air Force One while Mrs. Kennedy stood by his side. The days that followed had everyone glued to the TV set. We watched the funeral procession, and listened to the eerie drumbeats while little John-John saluted his daddy's casket going by. Our hearts were broken to see him, his sister Caroline, and especially Mrs. Kennedy. It was most tragic. The nation mourned along with them.

Around this time, the U.S. had only a supporting role in Vietnam, but as hundreds of our GIs were killed, our involvement intensified. As a military family, we were concerned because rumors increased that we would be sucked into the war to help the South Vietnamese. The sudden change in world events affected many military families, and the disturbing news affected me greatly.

Whenever I had some free time, I read. I developed an interest in studying as many religions as possible. I wanted to gain insight as to why there were so many different kinds. I began reading the Bible from cover to cover. Later, being curious about Joseph Smith and his revelations, I read the Book of Mormon. I read about Buddhism, the Jewish faith, and the varied Protestant faiths. Having been raised a Catholic, I ended up more confused than ever.

In wanting to understand the turmoil we lived in, my curiosity led me to read books by Ruth Montgomery. Her search on the subject of life after death fascinated me. I discovered other books about psychic phenomena, including several books written about Edgar Casey, the sleeping prophet. Each book helped strengthen my belief that there is indeed life after death. I was comfortable in my belief that the experiences I had as a child with my spiritual guardian and my most recent vision in the hospital were not figments of my imagination. Knowing that other people had similar experiences helped me understand that the reason we can communicate with God, his angels, and spirits is because our thoughts contain a separate brainwave, similar to radio waves, causing "mind transference."

Time suddenly became an obsession. I tried to make every moment count. With this new outlook, I consciously made the most of each day and became even more productive. I thrived on trying to accomplish as much as I could, and my energy level had no bounds. I truly felt like I was being guided. I formed the habit of saying a prayer before I started a painting to ask for inspiration. When I tapped into this great source, my work took on unexplainable results.

As an example, the mother of a friend of mine asked me to do a painting for her while she was visiting. I asked her what subject matter she would like. She replied, "Whatever you do will be fine because I love your work."

I did not know her very well and told her I would do something special when the mood struck me. Several weeks went by before I felt the urge to start her painting. After saying a silent prayer, I set up my easel and began painting. Without a plan or an idea, I started to paint, and a lovely snow scene emerged. That surprised me because, living in Texas, snow was the furthest thing from my mind. As I studied what I had painted, I decided it needed something more. In the distance, I painted a frozen pond with ice skaters on it. After that, I decided it did not need anything else. Content that it was finished, I let it dry for a few days and continued to study it every time I walked by it, looking to see if there was anything else I could add to improve it. When I determined there was nothing more I could do, I arranged to meet with Mrs. Montgomery at her house the next day. I was nervous about showing her the painting because it was so different from what I normally painted. I hoped she would like it. Since it was a commission, I needed her approval in order to collect my fee. As soon as I uncovered the painting, Mrs. Montgomery, who was eighty-two years old, exclaimed, "Oh, my God! You painted the back yard of my home where I grew up in Indiana! We used to ice skate on that pond every winter. It was always my favorite place during my childhood. I have so many fond memories of the fun times I spent there. How in the world did you know about that pond?"

All I could say was that it had just developed as I painted. I smiled, knowing I had tapped into the infinite source of divine inspiration once again.

I often found that I did my best work when I allowed my intuition to take over. There were times when I felt my hands were doing the work without my being aware of what I was painting. Several times, I noticed that I was painting without looking at the canvas or the watercolor paper. Like a piano player who plays without looking at the keys, artists enter into that unexplainable "zone" as well. I believe not only artists but everyone who is inspired to create something enters the dimension that inspires their best performance or work.

Another very unusual and interesting painting developed in the same way. The year was 1967. The war in Vietnam had escalated, and daily the news we heard on television was disturbing. One night, while Art was pulling his mandatory duty on the base, I was awakened from a sound sleep with an urgent need to paint. I looked at the clock and saw it was two o'clock in the morning. This had never happened to me before, but the urge was so strong, I felt I had to get up. I went to the kitchen and immediately set up my easel and paints. I began painting in a state of frenzy on a large 20" x 36" Masonite board. First, one oriental face appeared, and then another, until there were many faces of women and children with pain, agony, and fear expressed on their faces. In the forefront was a woman holding what appeared to be a dead baby in her arms. Above all the faces was a man's hand holding a dagger dripping with blood. In the lower right-hand corner, I had painted the Ten Commandments, with the sixth, "Thou Shalt Not Kill" dripping blood onto the middle cross I had painted below the tablets. The entire painting was done within an hour, without any conscious thought on my part. It was as if someone else had painted it for me. When I finished, I did not understand the painting and went to bed exhausted.

The next day, I showed Art the painting. He too could not understand why I had painted such a disturbing scene. My friend June came to visit later in the day. When I showed her the painting, her immediate reaction was shock. "Why on earth did you paint such a disturbing scene? It is so unlike your work. I can't bear to even look at it," she exclaimed.

The following February, in 1968, a picture appeared in the newspaper with similarities so pronounced that the message was clearly revealed to me. It was indeed a revelation from God in the middle of the night. The article read, "Bewilderment of war written on faces of Vietnam refugees . . . they huddle in fear in a village north of Hue during conflict in that area."

The oriental faces were nearly the same as the ones on my canvas. Even the woman holding the limp child in the foreground was in the same location. I was so shocked by the article that I saved it.

More tragedy struck. On April 4, 1968, Martin Luther King was assassinated. Two months later, on June 5, Senator Robert Kennedy was murdered. The world had gone mad it seemed, and riots were taking place everywhere. Young people were increasingly protesting against the war in Vietnam. Smoking marijuana had become a serious problem. As more and more people became addicted to the weed, still others became addicted to heroin.

My generation had not seen this type of behavior before. Many parents were bewildered and felt helpless. During this period, Art came home one day, and during our private time together, he told me he had declined an assignment to Hawaii. We had heard from some of his friends who had returned from Hawaii that teenagers in that area were running wild and were involved with drugs big time.

He was faced with making a serious decision to either risk being sent to Vietnam or put in for retirement from the air force. We spent all our evenings discussing our options. Two years before, Art had been promoted to Lieutenant Colonel, so we knew another promotion was not possible in the near future. He concluded that it was time for him to retire. The following month, he notified his commanding officer of his decision.

19

UNEXPECTED TRAGEDY

The decision to retire had not been an easy one, especially after having spent all our married life in the air force. Our first priority was to begin looking for a house in San Antonio, where we planned to live. Art immediately went on job interviews, knowing he would need the extra income to supplement his retirement pay. Wanting to locate in an area that would have excellent schools for Debbie and Arty, we found the perfect neighborhood in a brand new development in just a few days.

For the first time in my life, I was able to see the house as it was being built, from the foundation to the rooftop. I selected an English Tudor design for the outside. The inside décor gave me the greatest joy as I picked out the light fixtures, wallpaper, carpets, and every other necessity that went into the house.

By the time the house was finished, Art had found a job. St Mary's University hired him as the Director of Placement. It was a position that enabled him to work directly with students who wanted to find jobs upon graduation. Because he was a lieutenant colonel, we continued to enjoy a carefree lifestyle, and with the added income, we lived comfortably. At last we had the stability of a house that we would live in for the next thirty years.

While the movers were unpacking our belongings, our backyard neighbors, Margarite and Mario, came to welcome us with a pitcher of martinis and a full dinner on a tray. Margarite was my size, and we looked so much alike, we could have been sisters. Mario, a Colonel in the army, was still on active duty and stationed at Fort Sam Houston. After we became close friends, one favorite pastime Margarite and I enjoyed was having lunch at the Officer's Club. We did many other things together, and she became my best friend. Through the years, we developed a bond that has lasted to this day. Several of the other neighbors were friendly, and we formed close relationships with them as well. At last, the children could make lasting friends.

We enrolled Linda at Southwest Texas State College in San Marcos, located close to San Antonio, making it possible for her to come home on weekends. As a child, Linda had dreamed about becoming a schoolteacher, and now she was actually pursuing that career choice.

Debbie, a freshman in high school, was a straight-A student. She was involved in every extracurricular activity she could take on and excelled in everything she did. She tried out for the pep squad and made it. The following year she became a cheerleader. Her days were packed with fun and excitement, and she never turned down a challenge. Her leadership qualities were evident even then.

Arty, on the other hand, was not a leader type. He was shy and did not like crowds or organized groups. He was content to have one or two close friends to chum around with. He made good grades in junior high, but he had to study hard to maintain them. It amazed me to see how children reared in the same family could be so different.

I loved my children and wanted them to have everything that I did not have as a child. I admit we spoiled them in many ways, but we taught them to do what was right and we instilled in them the importance of morals, fairness, and honesty. I encouraged them to visualize what they wanted. This was a knowledge I had discovered and practiced. I explained that through concentration, a form of meditation, if they visualized the results of what they wanted to achieve, their subconscious mind would help them achieve it. More than once, I saw them achieve their goal. It surprised them whenever it happened.

I had taught art lessons two evenings and two afternoons per week at the Arts and Craft's Center at Randolph the entire time we lived on base. Now I continued giving classes there even after we moved. I joined several art organizations in the area and became a charter member to help establish the Randolph Art League and the Randolph Art Gallery in Universal City. I stayed busy serving as art chairman or vice president of several art groups. My career blossomed as I exhibited in galleries, entered juried competitions, and taught art classes.

Even though we were extremely busy, Art and I took on active roles in our neighborhood church. Two years later, Art was elected lay leader. He was extremely busy with his work at the university, yet he accepted the position of president with the Personnel and Management Association of the southwest. Before we knew it, it was 1970.

That year, Linda married a young man she had dated in high school. I revived my sewing skills and made her wedding dress and the bridesmaids' dresses and veils. Mother flew to San Antonio to help me with the many wedding preparations. It was a proud and happy moment when we watched Linda walk down the aisle, looking beautiful and radiant.

Shortly afterwards, Debbie registered at Southwest Texas State in San Marcos. Her major was in education with the goal of becoming a teacher, her life long ambition. Arty also planned to attend SWTSU when he finished high school. The years that followed were filled with countless events that kept us busy and made the time fly by.

Our New Year's Eve party in 1973 was as festive as ever, with our house filled to capacity with many friends. Art and I realized we were approaching the empty-nest phase of our lives and often discussed our future plans. We envisioned our first golf vacation for the following summer and looked forward to our time alone.

In mid July, Art presided over a breakfast meeting with the Personnel and Management Group. During the meeting, some of the members were having a heated debate over controversial issues, and Art had to act as the mediator. The morning was upsetting. He went to work after the meeting, and when he arrived at his office, he told his secretary he had been having terrible indigestion. She gave him some antacid tablets, and in a short time, he began to feel better.

Later in the afternoon, the minister of our church went to see Art at his office. He had never done that before, so Art was surprised when the minister told him he wanted to discuss a problem that involved the youth choir. The youth choir wanted to take a trip to Canada, but the finance committee had voted to use all the funds coming in for the next two years exclusively for a new fellowship hall being built. Since Art was the lay leader and the minister was the Youth Choir Director, he wanted Art to use his influence to change the vote. Art did not want to be part of this divisive intrigue and told the minister he would resign as lay leader rather than get involved. The minister said he would call a special board meeting at the church that night and begged Art to attend, saying he would announce that Art was taking a sabbatical for one year. Art told him no, that he intended to announce his resignation at the meeting.

When he came home after work, he complained about having had indigestion all day and did not feel like eating dinner. He left shortly after to attend the board meeting at the church. Within thirty minutes, he was back home and extremely angry. He told me the minister had accused him in front of the board members of being the instigator of a plot to stop the youth from going on the trip to Canada. While Art explained to the group how the minister had come to his office that afternoon and repeated what he had asked him to do, he started having excruciating chest pains. He pressed against his chest, hoping the feeling would go away, but when the pain intensified, he was barely able to get up and leave the meeting.

As he was telling me what happened, someone rang our doorbell. Art did not want me to answer the door because he knew it would be someone from the meeting, or worse yet, the minister with some lame excuse. He did not want to talk about it anymore because it upset him too much. The person at the door was persistent and kept pressing the doorbell. Unable to listen to that ringing any longer, I answered the door. To my relief, it was one of Art's best friends, Bob, who looked downright pale with worry. Without a word, Bob pushed past me and ran to Art, saying, "Hey, buddy. How do you feel? You scared the heck out of me. When you left the meeting, you were as pale as a sheet. I came by to make sure you were all right."

Art was relieved to see that it wasn't the minister. He relaxed and started to discuss what had happened. Before too long, the rest of the board members came to the house. As the conversation began to get heated with the retelling of what had been said and was repeated over and over, Art could not tolerate it any longer. He began to sweat and groan because of severe chest pains. He clutched his chest and said it felt like an elephant was sitting on it. As a group, we knew he might be having a heart attack. Several people had to help him get into the back seat of one of the cars, and I sat next to him, trying to comfort him. During the entire drive to the hospital at Fort Sam Houston, Art was unable to sit still and groaned constantly from the excruciating pain. I knew this was serious because my intuition warned me that I must prepare for some difficult times ahead.

When we arrived at the hospital, a nurse took Art to the emergency room and another nurse told us to sit in the hall and wait. We waited for over an hour without seeing anyone. Finally, I went to the room where they had taken Art and found him in one of the cubicles. He was sitting on the cot fully dressed. When he saw me, he jumped down and said, "Let's get the hell out of here! I've been sitting here all this time and haven't seen a doctor yet. They've been walking by seeing other patients, and nobody has bothered to even come in the room to ask me why I'm here. My pain has finally gone away. I feel fine, so let's go home."

On our way out, a doctor stopped us and asked what the problem was. Art made light of his pain, so the doctor told him to go home and rest. He gave him some nitroglycerin tablets and told him to put one under his tongue if the pain came back. If the pain persisted, he said he should come back to the emergency room. Our friends were appalled, but nobody could convince Art to stay. He practically ran out of the hospital, he was that angry.

When we got home, I had to help him get out of the car and into the house. From a robust person, he was reduced to a helpless invalid. Yet, he was in a state of denial. Feeling exhausted, he went to bed as soon as we entered the house. I lay next to him fully clothed because I felt a sense of foreboding. My intuition was telling me to be prepared, that I might have to rush him back to the hospital during the night. Unable to sleep, I spent the night thinking of what I should do in the morning.

After a sleepless night, I called my friend Helen first thing in the morning. She was a nurse in the cardiac ICU ward at Fort Sam. I told her what had happened the night before and described Art's symptoms. With concern in her voice, she gave me the name of the head cardiologist and his phone number. She insisted I call him right away, not to wait. As soon as we hung up, I called him. When I told him what had happened in the emergency room the night before, he was horrified and furious. He told me to bring Art to the hospital as soon as possible. I tried to help him get dressed, but he insisted on taking a shower first.

When he came out of the shower, he was barely able to walk to the bedroom. The least amount of effort zapped whatever strength he had. By the time I helped him into the car, he was perspiring profusely and having difficulty breathing. I prayed all the way to the hospital fearing he would die before I got there.

The doctor I had spoken to was waiting for us by the emergency entrance. After a brief talk in his office, he insisted that Art be admitted to the Intensive Care Unit immediately. He told us they would have to run some tests to determine what his condition was before deciding how to treat him.

I followed them to the ICU on the second floor and helped Art get undressed. After putting him to bed, the nurse gave me his clothes and other personal items to take home. I was told to leave. I would be allowed to visit him only during visiting hours because the patients in that unit needed constant supervision and rest.

When I got home, I removed his clothing from the paper bag and hung it up. As I pulled out his wallet and held it in my hand, a vision flashed in my mind. I saw a hearse with a procession behind it going along a road that entered a cemetery. I had the distinct premonition that Art was going to die.

Later that afternoon, our minister was allowed to visit him in ICU because they allowed the clergy admittance at any time. At three o'clock, just as the minister was leaving the room, Art had a massive heart attack. The doctor called me after they had him stabilized. When I heard the news, my heart beat so fast I thought I would have a heart attack myself. I was told to hurry because they were not sure if they could save him. I broke all speeding rules and got to the hospital without being stopped. By the time I arrived, Art was resting comfortably, but the doctor told me he had severe heart damage. I was allowed to see him only for a short time.

As he held my hand, he told me what had happened. The minister had come by to apologize for what he had said at the meeting the night before and asked Art to please forgive him. Art told the minister his treachery had hurt him very much, but he forgave him. They both cried, since they had been closer than brothers for many years, and after a short conversation, they prayed together. The last thing Art remembered was seeing the minister leave the room, then an agonizing pain in his chest before losing consciousness.

Art had always been a doubting Thomas, and he surprised me with an amazing story. When he was in-between worlds, he said, he saw his mother, his father, and other deceased relatives. They were standing in front of a building that was surrounded by a blinding golden light. In fact, it was so bright that it was difficult to look at them. Their arms were outstretched, motioning for him to go with them. He said he was really tempted to follow them, but he kept hearing his name being called out in the distance. As he focused on his name, he entered a brightly lit tunnel. The light made him travel at a speed beyond description. Then, he heard a distinctly deep voice telling him he must go back. He was convinced that it was God speaking to him. When he opened his eyes, he felt the doctor slapping his face while repeating, "Art, wake up! Art, come back! Art, wake up!"

After that experience, he believed his mission was to return to earth to tell me what he had seen and heard. He wanted me to know that I had been right all along. That he remembered hearing God's voice revealing many things to him. Mainly that our souls do live on after we die. I was shocked to hear him say these things in such an urgent and convincing way.

During our marriage, my beliefs had been a source of some of our most heated arguments. Ever since my vision in Virginia, I tried to tell him about our spiritual and human sides, but we always ended up having a heated argument. After several years, I decided not to bring up the subject of my beliefs and my vision, since it did not make sense to him. I could hardly believe I was now listening to Art say how sorry he was that he had ridiculed me so many times before and had made fun of my beliefs in front of the children. Listening to what he was telling me now was a shock, especially coming from such a big doubter. His encounter with God was an unbelievable revelation to me.

By the time I arrived home and parked my car, a flower truck pulled up in front of the house. The driver came to the door holding a flower vase containing a single red rose with baby's breath. This had always been Art's special gift to me on our anniversary and on my birthdays. I wondered what in the world this could mean. The attached card said, "I will always love you, my darling, even from afar."

This made me realize he knew he was dying.

One week later, I was awakened at three o'clock in the morning. Art had suffered another massive heart attack. This time, they were unable to save him. My world fell apart. Even breathing was difficult. I don't remember driving to the hospital or calling Debbie at school. I was like a robot, moving without a brain, completely detached from my body. The next few weeks became a blur as each day was filled with necessary preparations. The day I had to go to the funeral home to pick out Art's casket was the most difficult day of my life. I did not want to leave the house. I knew it was the moment I dreaded most because it would be my moment of reality. I would have to accept the fact that he wasn't coming back.

Being my first time to enter a funeral home, the experience was traumatic. Mother had flown to San Antonio to help me as best she could, but I was unresponsive for many days. Debbie came home from school, and Arty was home also, but for the life of me, I don't remember much of anything that went on.

I was told that so many people attended the funeral that the church was packed to capacity. Chairs had to be placed in the entry foyer and on the front porch to accommodate the overflow. I knew Art had many friends and was loved by a lot of people. This response was certainly a great testimony. The heavy rain that came down in torrents did not deter anyone, and the procession to the cemetery was over a mile long. As we approached the cemetery, I noticed that it was the exact same route I had seen in my vision when I held Art's wallet.

The ladies of the church took care of feeding the people who came to the house afterwards. I was there in body only because, months later, I could not remember who came or what had transpired. I went through a full three months of amnesia, even though at the time, I felt I was in complete control. Becoming a widow at age forty-six was devastating. I had become so accustomed to the comfortable, affluent lifestyle we enjoyed that I never envisioned it would end abruptly. I kept remembering the many times we had talked about our retirement years. It was painful to realize that none of the things we had glowingly talked about doing together would ever happen.

Mother stayed with me for several months in order to be helpful. She at least made sure I ate. Had I been by myself, I know I would not have bothered to cook for myself or to eat at all. Whenever I closed my eyes, all I could see was the procession of cars driving along the road entering the cemetery. Reliving every detail of Art's heart attack, the weeks of agonizing visits to ICU, and the hours spent in prayer begging for his life to be spared, I was unable to sleep. Art's time to leave had come, and there was nothing we could do to change that. As the weeks went by, I lost interest in everything.

After the funeral, Linda returned to Maryland, where she lived. She was too far away to be of any comfort to me, and besides, I knew she was going through her own grieving process. Much to my regret, I was not able to help her. Debbie and Arty returned to school, and I was comforted in knowing that they, at least, were well established and would be consoled by their many friends. My mind was at peace about them. They both came home on weekends and tried to console me, but it was too soon. Nothing they said or did was enough to bring me out of my depression. Later on, I felt guilty because I had not been there for them.

Many days, I did not want to get dressed or even get out of bed. I preferred to stay covered up to my neck with several blankets because the warmth was somehow comforting. Being in our bed made it seem like Art was close by. I stared at the walls until sleep overtook my numb senses. I was alive in body, but my spirit was in limbo, as if part of me was going through a transformation.

During the next four months, I was able to overcome my grief mostly through the efforts of many friends. Mainly though, it was through prayer and the comforting thoughts I received from my unseen guardian. He reminded me that Art was gone only from the earth plane, that even though he was in another dimension, we could still communicate with each other with our thoughts, the same way we use our thoughts to pray.

One day I was reminded about what Art had told me while he was in the hospital, after he was made aware that we all live on after death. He told me that if he should die, he would come back somehow to let me know his spirit still lived on.

We had a dog named Cristie that we had given to Arty for his thirteenth birthday. She was a hyperactive beagle who chewed on furniture, shoes, and whatever else she fancied. Because of that, Art did not want her in the house, so she stayed in the backyard all the time. Now that Art was no longer with us, I decided to bring Cristie in the house to be a companion for me. She was a comfort and was really my dog anyway, since I had cared for her from the time we brought her home as a puppy.

We had a black leather recliner with an ottoman in the family room. It was Art's chair. The minute he came home, he would sit in that chair. No one dared sit in it, not even when he was away. I usually sat on the couch on the opposite side of the room to watch TV. Now that Cristie was staying inside with me, I placed a blanket on the couch next to me so she could lie close to my body.

One night, three months after Art had died, I was sitting on the couch watching television with Cristie at my side when she suddenly stood up on her four legs and began barking at the black recliner. I could tell she was afraid to jump down from the couch. She ran circles on the couch, growling and baring her teeth in a ferocious way. All of a sudden, she jumped down from the couch and made a beeline for the recliner, ready to attack, barking and growling while she stared at the chair. Then she ran across the room and stood in the entrance of our bedroom door, afraid to go inside. She stood there with her hind leg in an attack position, her fur standing up while she growled with her teeth exposed and barked incessantly. I could not make her stop. Getting off the couch, I turned the light on in the bedroom, but that did not deter her either. I finally had to put her outside to keep her quiet.

About a month later, I was in bed sound asleep when I was awakened by the mattress being pushed down, the way Cristie did when she wanted me to let her go outside to pee. It was three in the morning, and being half asleep, I did not want to get up. I said, "Oh, Cristie, go back to bed. I'm too tired to get up."

I tried to go back to sleep, when again, I was awakened by the mattress being pressed down, only harder and faster this time. Now awake and disgruntled, I got up, saying, "All right, Cristie. Come on."

I expected her to be at the back door, ready to make a mad dash, but when I entered the family room, I saw her on the couch not only sleeping soundly but also snoring! I immediately thought of Art. He had found a way to get through to me in a way that I would know it was him.

In December, I went to California with Linda and her husband so I would not be alone for Christmas. Luckily, Debbie had plans for the holidays with her boyfriend and other school friends and said she did not mind staying home to take care of the house and Cristie. When I returned from California, Debbie told me something very scary had happened while I was away. She was hesitant at first and somewhat unsure if she should even tell me. She finally worked up the courage to tell me that while she was sound asleep one night, she felt her mattress being pushed down. Without hesitating, she got up to let Cristie out, since she knew that was her way of letting us know she wanted to go out. Her bedroom was on the second floor, so she ran downstairs to open the backdoor for Christie. But as she entered the family room, there was Cristie on the couch sound asleep and snoring! This meant she had been asleep the entire time. When I told her of my same experience, we both knew that Art was trying to let us know he was with us in spirit. It could only be him.

Within a month of Art's death, I faced a new problem. My income was reduced to less than half of what Art had been making. I was shocked when I learned that my portion of his retirement pay would be six hundred dollars per month. He did have a small life insurance policy with the VA and one from the university. Combined, they would barely be enough to last more than a year.

I had to find another source of income. Good gosh, the mortgage payment alone was half that amount, plus I had many other household expenses, car expenses, and several insurance payments to be made monthly. That would leave me with barely enough money for food and other expenses. I immediately put myself on a budget. Having learned how to conserve when I was single made that part easy. It was clear, though, that I had to find a way to supplement my income right away.

20

SELF-REALIZATION

I toyed with the idea of going into interior decorating, but after checking out the requirements, I found it would involve one year of schooling followed by another year of on the job training. Common sense told me it would take too long before I would start earning a decent salary. Time being of the essence, I determined my solution would be to become more dedicated to my art career and start thinking of ways to sell more paintings. I had built up a sizeable inventory and knew that if I painted on a regular basis, I would have enough to sell to supplement my income.

In the meantime, one of my art patrons, a Mr. Kline, was part owner of the best real estate company in San Antonio. It was named Rosow and Kline. He had often mentioned to me that a lot of money was made in the real estate business. I decided to have a talk with him at my next art show, which was scheduled in a few weeks. I stayed busy framing my new work, and I looked forward to the big event that took place every year on the banks of the River Walk in San Antonio.

When Mr. and Mrs. Kline came by my display, they purchased another one of my watercolors. As soon as I sensed the right moment, I told Mr. Kline I was interested in going into real estate. He was sympathetic about my situation and very glad that I was contemplating this move. He offered to sponsor me and invited me to come by his office so we could discuss it further. The following week, I went to his office, and after listening to the job requirements, decided that was what I wanted to do.

That same day, I enrolled in a crash course being offered at a real estate school nearby. It was a four-month course with classes held every day. I learned that the state exam would follow a month later. If I passed it, I could be a licensed real estate agent within six months. This would not only help me learn about real estate but would also be an added benefit that would help me in my art career. The course and the books were expensive, but it was well worth it. I studied hard, wanting to attain my license as soon as possible.

My days and nights were so full that I did not have time to brood and dwell on my loneliness. I spent the mornings in class, feverishly taking notes, and the nights reviewing my notes and memorizing their content. My notes were so complete and extensive that the other students borrowed them from me. My next-door neighbor had been a close friend to Art, and he offered to help me with the math—the main subject I dreaded. He came to my house and grilled me for hours on fractions and complicated math problems that covered interest rates and the like. To make it easier, I invested in a calculator.

When I finished the course, I spent the next month studying because the state exam was coming up soon. When the notice came in the mail with the date of the exam, I nearly panicked because, having been out of school for so many years, I had no self-confidence. Two weeks later, the exam was given at one of the universities in a large auditorium-style classroom. The rows of seats numbered in the hundreds, and I chose to sit way up in the middle, where I could barely make out the instructor's face as he walked back and forth on the stage while giving us instructions.

My stomach churned, and my face flushed from worrying. It was through sheer determination that I was able to control my shaking hands. When we were told to begin, I took a deep breath, said a silent prayer, and regained my composure after answering the first few questions.

The test was in sections: law, measurements, contracts, etc. When I came to the math part, I pulled out my calculator. After the first problem, it quit working. The batteries had gone dead. It never occurred to me to check them before taking the test because I was not familiar with calculators. I had to finish the exam without it, relying on what I had stored in my brain. When I turned in my papers after reviewing them for possible errors, I noticed I had finished before many of the other people. When I walked in my house, I felt pretty good, even though there was a nagging unrest about whether or not I had passed.

Several weeks went by before the results were sent to my broker. He proudly told me that, not only had I passed, but my grade was a 97—almost a perfect score. Getting that certificate and my realtor pin was like graduating from college. I kept repeating, "I did it! I did it! I did it."

Without realizing it, I had joined the best real estate company in San Antonio. We were given intensive two-week training courses before being allowed to deal with any clients. Even agents who transferred from other companies were required to participate. During my first month on the job, I sold four houses.

Besides my real estate business, I continued giving art lessons two afternoons and two evenings per week at the arts and crafts center on the base. I had made it a practice long ago to not take on more than twelve students in each class. This made it possible for me to give individual attention to each student. As a result, my classes were always full and I had an ongoing waiting list.

During my free hours, I painted. I had always framed my own oil paintings, and now that I was painting in acrylic and watercolor, I learned to cut matte boards and framed each new painting myself. On weekends, I participated in art shows or set up one-person shows. They became my best source of sales for repeat business and commission requests.

Fourteen months flew by, and many changes took place. The previous December, Debbie had graduated with a degree in education and was immediately hired as a fourth grade teacher. She moved back home, and that really boosted my spirit. Having someone else in the house was less lonely, and having another person to eat with made life more pleasant.

The companionship made us even closer as mother and daughter. With my fluctuating income, I asked her to pay a small amount toward the food each month. I thought it was a good way to teach her about responsibility, just as my mother had taught me.

That same year, Linda was expecting her first child, and I flew to Maryland to be with her when the baby was expected. It was a boy—my first grandchild. He was the picture of health, with rosy cheeks, Linda's huge blue eyes, and copper-red hair. They named him Bryan.

The following year, I returned to Maryland when Linda's second child was born prematurely by six weeks. The baby was a girl they named Shelley. She was frail and tiny and had to be kept in an incubator for a few weeks, but she rallied, and within two months, became a healthy, beautiful girl.

The following year, being away from family, Linda decided to move back to Texas. She wanted to be close to me in San Antonio, but they located in Austin, where teaching opportunities were better. Debbie and I helped them get settled into a house we had found for rent, and within a few months, Linda was teaching again. Having my daughters close by was the best thing that could have happened that year.

Before long, Debbie became engaged to her college sweetheart, Cass. I was able to help her prepare for her big day, which was coming up in a few months, December 20, 1975. We shopped for her wedding dress together and found the perfect white satin and lace creation. This time, the bridesmaids and the flower girl bought their own dresses and shoes. Since the wedding was scheduled a few days before Christmas, Debbie selected Christmas red for her color scheme. She asked her brother Arty to walk her down the aisle and give her away in place of her dad. Even though Art was no longer with us, I knew he would want Debbie to have the most beautiful wedding any bride could wish for, just as he had done for Linda five years before. The lavish reception was held in the Hilton Hotel in San Antonio, with several hundred guests in attendance. The next day Debbie and Cass flew to Hawaii for a ten-day honeymoon.

When Debbie moved out after they returned, I was extremely lonely and found it hard to adjust. Sometimes I wandered from room to room, remembering the many events that had taken place in each one. My sadness continued until one morning I decided to meditate and renew contact with my spiritual guardian. I was reminded that my attitude had a lot to do with my state of mind, and I should concentrate on the wonderful things that were happening in my life. It felt like a great weight had been removed, and my renewed energy seemed to have no bounds. My real estate transactions began to explode, and I often worked past midnight. Many days, my dedicated efforts paid off, and I developed a client base that generated all the income I needed.

I converted the game room on the second floor into my art studio. The room was large enough to accommodate a couch and a coffee table. I arranged a sitting area to add some class to the room and then hung my certificates of awards on the walls. I bought a drafting table that fit perfectly below the window to give me the best light to paint by. Paintings began to flow onto canvases. Like a scientist in his laboratory, I tried new techniques. While painting, I entered into a meditative state and saw landscapes appear in my mind, then created them on my canvas.

For years, my friends had urged me to enter my paintings in some of the more prestigious art competitions. I had always been too busy, but now I felt my work would get more recognition if I took on this new challenge.

As I put the finishing touches on a 22" x 30" full sheet, D'Arches cold-press watercolor paper, my intuition told me that the landscape I had just finished was good enough to enter in the upcoming statewide watercolor competition. It depicted an island in the distance with an assortment of trees with autumn hues reflected in the water. I purposely left some of the white paper untouched below the water to give it a dramatic effect and titled it "Reflections."

Since this was my first entry in the Texas Watercolor Society competition, I was anxious to hear if it had been accepted. Eight hundred paintings were submitted, and only eighty-five would get selected. When I opened the notification card and learned I had been accepted in the show, I nearly fainted. An immense sense of gratitude came over me for the inspiration that had made it possible. Membership in the Texas Watercolor Society is open only to artists who have been accepted into one of their exhibits. I was now qualified to become a member!

Watercolor painting was my new passion, and I began to create a series of works featuring broken windows covered with dust. They sold like hotcakes. A friend named Lillian, who already owned six of my paintings, bought one and shared a funny story about it. She hung it in her master bathroom on the wall facing the commode. Her husband Rayford came running out of the bathroom one night and shouted, "You know, I wish you would move that painting. It's embarrassing for me to have Lucille looking at me the entire time I'm sitting on the john."

Lillian thought he had lost his mind and asked, "What in the world are you talking about?"

Rayford went to the bathroom and came back with the painting.

"Okay, see for yourself. Can't you see Lucille's reflection in the broken glass?"

She took a closer look, and to her astonishment, saw a perfect reflection of my face in the painted glass. She called to tell me what had happened, and I told her I had to see it for myself. We met for lunch the next day, and I couldn't believe what I saw. I had executed her painting the same way I had done all the others—applying white paint, rubbing some of it off, letting it dry, applying more white paint, and repeating the procedure many times while squinting to get the desired dirty-glass effect. How my likeness got captured in the dirty broken glass is a mystery to me, but sure enough, I was staring at my own reflection!

Membership in the art organizations I belonged to kept me busy attending monthly business meetings. The president of my favorite organization, the National Society of Arts and Letters, asked me to be the art chairman. Even though I knew it was going to be a lot of work, I accepted the position and felt a sense of excitement about the challenges it would present. The Society's National Convention was to be held in San Antonio that year, and our chapter was the sponsor. As art chairman, it would be my responsibility to spearhead the planning and organizing, including overseeing the artwork that would be shipped in from all over the country. The category of the competition was to be visual art done in watercolor that year. I recruited many member volunteers, who helped host the best-attended convention sponsored by the organization in many years.

Two years later, my friend Susan, who had sponsored me for membership, urged me to accept the nomination as president for the organization. She encouraged me and tried to convince me I was more qualified than I gave myself credit for. The familiar inner voice I had relied on all my life kept telling me I was ready. I held back and accepted the position of vice president instead. Another member named Jeanne was elected president. But my divine source evidently had other plans for me.

In June, Jeanne was diagnosed with a brain tumor and had to resign. As a result, I began getting countless phone calls urging me to accept the presidency. Feeling guilty about letting the organization down, I asked for guidance. Two weeks later, I accepted the nomination and was elected president.

Becoming president of the San Antonio chapter tested all of my talents and enhanced my self-esteem. With so many demands to speak at meetings, it truly helped me overcome my persistent shyness. Delegating tasks and following up on their implementation became second nature. I had to learn to work with the varied personalities that comprised my appointed committee chairpersons. Becoming a better public speaker was necessary in order to introduce the special guest speakers from different fields of art whom I had to introduce at the meetings. A banquet was held at the end of each year to award the scholarships we gave to the winners. It always involved a great deal of planning and a lot of work. My two-year commitment was filled with newsletter deadlines, luncheons, competitions, and conventions. The following two years, I served as National Art Chairman for the organization. But none of this truly filled the void in my life.

* * *

Art had been gone nearly two years when I met a woman named Jackie, who worked at one of the title companies that handled my real estate closings. Sipping coffee while we waited for a client who was late for his appointment, we discovered that we had much in common and began meeting for dinner. When I was with her, we laughed all the time. I admired her carefree spirit. Jackie had been divorced for as long as I had been a widow.

One night she told me about a singles' club she had heard about that had been formed mainly for professional men and women. They held dances every Friday night, and she suggested we go sometime. I promised I would think about it, but just thinking about it made me uneasy. The following Friday, I had an unusually bad day at work. Feeling sad and dejected, I called Jackie. After venting my frustrations I said, "You know what? How about going to the dance tonight? I'm ready to go out and have some fun. I miss dancing, and I want to meet new people."

She screamed so loud I nearly dropped the phone. She kept repeating, "Oh, my God. Oh, my God. You really want to go? I can't believe it! This is terrific! I'll be at your house at seven o'clock to pick you up."

While getting dressed, my hands were sweating and I didn't think I would ever get them dry. I was thinking about my first venture out and the fact that I was going to date again. I took my time selecting what to wear and decided on my current favorite rust-colored velour dress with matching shoes. Gold loop earrings and a gold choker completed the outfit.

When Jackie arrived, I settled into the front seat of her car, and like two high school teenagers, we began giggling. With her foot on the accelerator, she yelled, "Let's go!"

When we entered the dance hall, the DJ was playing one of my favorite songs: "For the Good Times." An enthusiastic group of people who were the official greeters was standing in the entrance, so Jackie and I introduced ourselves as newcomers. We were encouraged to mingle with the crowd or find a table of our choice if we wanted to sit. We opted to stand by the edge of the dance floor, where it seemed the majority of the people had gathered.

A new dance tune started playing, and a dark-haired man in his mid fifties walked over in our direction, took Jackie by the hand, and pulled her onto the dance floor, saying, "Let's dance." She was surprised at the way he had led her onto the floor, but she looked back at me with a big grin on her face. Her eyes gleamed as they disappeared onto the crowded dance floor.

I stood there like a wallflower through several dances before anyone even approached me. I was beginning to feel like a fool and decided I had made a terrible mistake. A few minutes later, a man came from behind, tapped me on my right shoulder, and said, "Care to dance?"

The suddenness of his pull toward the dance floor nearly made me trip over my own feet. We glided across the floor as if we had danced together for many years. He complimented me on how well I danced and said he wanted to dance with me the rest of the night because he was enjoying himself. I was delighted to be kept on the dance floor until intermission.

Later on one of the regular ladies told me he was known as the best dancer in the place and that he liked to approach newcomers and test them on the dance floor. After a few weeks, he would start an affair that would end in a very short time. That was fine with me. My only interest was dancing and having a reason to get out of the house.

At one of the dances, Jackie met Travis. He was a tall Texan with salt-and-pepper hair tied in a long ponytail in the back. His deep-set eyes squinted as if they held a secret. In no time at all, they began dating exclusively, and Jackie found out that not all divorced men were "scumbags." Travis turned out to be a true gentleman. He was proud to say he was a native Texan, born in Bandera, a small town west of San Antonio that still resembled the Old West. I could see why Jackie fell madly in love with him after only a few dates. They were so much alike. Six months later, they married and moved to California. That was a match made in heaven. I lost a good friend, but my intuition told me she had come into my life to teach me to laugh and to be happy again. After that, I was more carefree and less reserved.

I continued going to the dances nearly every Friday night by myself. One night, a man walked in who was new to the group. He was so nice-looking that he literally took my breath away. He stood over six feet tall, had curly gray hair, and a build like a male model you'd see in a magazine. I noticed that the attraction was mutual when, with a deep voice with a Texas accent, he said to me, "Hello, little lady. My name is Del. What might your name be?"

After I introduced myself, he took my right hand and kissed the back of it, like European men do. I was surprised and told him, "You'd better go inside because the band is about to take a break. Intermission will start as soon as they finish this number."

He grinned, baring his perfect white teeth, and replied, "Nope, I'd rather stay here and talk with you, if that's all right."

He informed me it was the first time he had gone to a singles' dance, and he was more interested in talking with me. I guess we were a sight together since, even in my two-inch heels, Del towered over me. He made quite a stir with the ladies. As we walked by, their gaze took in his most unusual gray eyes and well-cropped wavy hair.

Before intermission was over, he suggested that we leave in order to get better acquainted in a quieter atmosphere. I accepted, and we decided to meet at a Jim's Restaurant close by. I arrived first and watched for him by the entrance. As he approached, I noticed he was wearing a rawhide jacket and blue jeans. He looked as if he had just stepped out of a western movie set. We got comfortable in a booth and ordered coffee. Our conversation lasted for two hours. We reluctantly said goodnight and parted with a handshake.

Del called me at home the next night, and I invited him over for coffee. The weeks that followed were no longer boring; we saw each other nearly every night. Our time together was spent with Del telling me about many unusual Texas customs and pertinent facts about Texas history. Eventually, when he showed interest in my art career, I was hooked.

Del enjoyed helping me set up my art shows and would do anything to please me. At last, I had found someone who would load the paintings in the truck, help set up the exhibit, and take down the paintings afterwards. I had done all that by myself for many years, so it was a welcome change. Art had been supportive of my art career, but he had never wanted to help me set up my exhibits because he was too busy with his own interests.

Del became a wonderful companion. He took me to the Davis Mountains and Fort Stockton, on the way to El Paso. We went to Palo Duro Canyon several times, an area similar to the Grand Canyon, only on a smaller scale. We travelled all over Texas to visit historical sights, stopping along the way to take pictures of unusual landscapes and spend time in many quaint towns.

We dated for three fun-filled years. Then I began seeing signs that something was amiss. A nagging feeling was warning me, but I tried to ignore it. He started flirting openly with cashiers and waitresses, something he had never done before. I thought at first he was just being friendly.

During our courtship, I had never gone to Del's house without him being at home, even though he had often encouraged me to do so and had shown me where he kept a key hidden. One afternoon, after shopping close to his house, I had a strong urge to use the bathroom. I decided his house was the closest place I could get to, and knowing he was not home, I let myself in. I ran to the master bedroom to use the bathroom, and after washing my hands, stepped back into the bedroom. I spotted a picture on the dresser, and out of curiosity, I picked it up. Wow! What a shock to see a nude woman lying on her back in an explicit sexual pose. From the furniture and room layout, I knew it was a recent photograph taken in the room where I stood.

I grabbed my purse and was ready to run out the door when I heard Del's truck pull up in the driveway. There was no need to run. Having seen my car parked in front of his house, he knew I was inside. I sat on the couch, put the picture in my pocket, and waited for him to come inside. He came running toward me saying, "What's wrong, darlin'? Are you all right? Did something happen?"

Without saying a word, I lifted the picture from my pocket and handed it to him. He began talking fast.

"Where did you get that? That's a picture of my ex-wife that I took a long time ago before we were divorced!"

"Oh, really," I said. "Well, how come it says Jan on the back? That's not your ex-wife's name!"

Taking the picture from me, he looked on the back, and then lowered his eyes. He was forced to admit that it was not his ex, that it was Jan, the minister's wife where he attended church.

We went to different churches on Sunday, and then we'd meet for lunch afterwards. Several times in the past three months, he had been late. He explained that the minister's wife had engaged him in a conversation after the service to discuss problems she was having in her marriage. At the time, I told him I understood. But, when it happened several more times, I told him she should seek a counselor, that he was not an authority on the subject of divorce or marriage.

After seeing the picture, I knew their relationship was more than talks in the parking lot after church. I gathered the few things I had left at his house during our time together, and as I approached the front door, I felt pangs of sadness, realizing that this beautiful man whom I had enjoyed precious moments with was also a deceiver. Without saying goodbye, I walked out, knowing it would be the last time I would ever see him.

I later remembered that people come into our lives for specific reasons. I did discover love again. Del had taught me many interesting facts about Texas that would help me later on. During our time together, I became carefree and was happy for three wonderful years.

One day as I recalled this period in my life, a poem came to me.

Self-Realization

You must know sorrow in order to know joy
To have been seared with hurts and grief
Time tempered with alacrity of fire
Yet emerging unscathed is a test of character,
Sustaining those in life who emerge stronger
Wiser in thought, more generous in feeling,
For his brothers and sisters who are frail
In patience and wisdom
Count not the years of hardship and despair
As wasted years,
For the lessons learned during these periods
Make you the "giant" of today
With strength untold
To carry you through life's engaging battles
With situations and challenges
Occurring daily to mold you
Into the complete "I" of self-realization.

Around this time, Debbie was teaching fourth grade and expecting her first child. At night, she went to classes in San Marcos to take courses towards a master's degree in administration. Several months after her daughter Rebecca was born, she received her master's with high honors. Debbie served as an assistant principal for quite a few years, and eventually became a principal. Later in her career, the Austin Independent School District recognized her and honored her as Administrator of the Year.

Three years after Rebecca was born, Debbie gave birth to a son they named Robert. I now had six grandchildren.

21

MEETING BILL

Having my family close by was invigorating and completed my life. We established the tradition of celebrating individual birthdays, and once again, were together for Christmas and Thanksgiving, just like in the old days. My grandchildren were now a big part of my happiness.

Every year, my mother and her husband George came to visit for the entire month of July. Our days were filled with dinner parties, travel to interesting places, such as the Natural Bridge Caverns near New Braunfels, the Missions around San Antonio, and the abundant tourist sites. Once in awhile, Mother and Papa George came back and spent Christmas with us as well. Even Aunt Lucy came to visit nearly every year for a week in the summer, and once in awhile for Christmas. I encouraged other family members to visit us and can't recall how many times I visited the Alamo with all of them.

The only person missing was my son Arty. He had moved to Denver, Colorado, after attending college for one year in San Marcos. A car parts distributor hired him as an inventory controller. After being in Denver six months, he met the love of his life, Peggy. She was divorced with two little girls, Galatea, seven, and Heidi, six.

Traveling to Austin to help with the grandchildren now and then was becoming a problem. On my way back home from Austin one day, it dawned on me that I should move to Austin. As the idea gained momentum, I thought of all the changes the move would necessitate. I would have to give up my well-established art career and terminate my membership in several organizations that were important to me. It was a difficult decision to make. In the end, I decided that being close to my daughters and my four young grandchildren was more important.

Around this time, the election of President Jimmy Carter had taken place. During his term, interest rates soared to unprecedented heights, which affected the real estate market. As the economy continued to spiral downward and interest rates climbed to fifteen and twenty percent, it made sense to end my career as a real estate agent. My last transaction was to sell my house in San Antonio and purchase one in Austin.

One of the first commitments I took on after I settled in my new house was to help establish a chapter of the National Society of Arts and Letters in Austin. I agreed to be the liaison with the San Antonio Chapter and the National Chapter. The Austin members were professors from The University of Texas, professional retired artists in all fields of art, and several board members of the Austin symphony. The meetings were held once a month in the home of one of the members.

At one of the meetings, I met a member named Emily, who happened to be an art agent. After we became better acquainted, she sought me out at one of the meetings and told me she was interested in seeing my work, that she was considering representing me. After a lengthy discussion, we arranged to meet at her house the following week. I was told to bring a portfolio with some of my watercolor paintings and a few framed acrylics.

The following Thursday, we spent several hours going over my work, and I answered Emily's many questions about my art career and accomplishments. She was impressed and decided to become my agent. Emily asked me to leave my portfolio of paintings, saying she was going to Galveston in a few days and was meeting with the owner of an art gallery on the Strand. She felt certain he would want to handle my work in his gallery.

When she returned a week later, she was happy to report that the owner liked my work, since he specialized in watercolor paintings. He told her he wanted to have at least five more of my watercolors because he needed several in reserve in order to switch my display fairly often. Then Emily shocked me by saying she did not want to continue as my agent, that it would be too time-consuming to have to drive to Galveston to exchange my paintings as they sold. She urged me to contact the owner as soon as possible and inform him that I would be dealing with him personally. I was surprised when she refused to accept a commission on future sales or to take any compensation for the time she had already spent on my behalf.

Wanting to give myself time to think about the implications this would entail, I waited a few days before calling the gallery. A week later, I dialed the phone number, and a male voice answered. "Howland Gallery, may I help you?"

The sound of a very deep voice took me by surprise. I told him who I was and that Emily had given me his name and had encouraged me to call him personally for any future business dealings. He remembered their conversation and said he was pleased to hear from me. He asked me to repeat my name and said his name was Bill Howland but asked me to call him Bill. We kept the conversation brief and discussed my bringing more paintings to his gallery the following week. I had to ask one of my male friends if he would go with me because I feared having to drive through the center of Houston, an area I was not familiar with and dreaded. I asked my friend Chuck to drive me down the following Friday, and he was pleased to be able to do me the favor.

When we walked into the gallery, I was impressed with the way it was decorated and arranged. After brief introductions, I began showing Bill my work. We were involved for the next three hours switching paintings, taking some out of frames, and replacing them with others. My friend Chuck took on the time-consuming job for me. Bill later had me sign a contract, agreeing to the gallery terms.

Before leaving, Bill extended an invitation for me to come to Galveston anytime and said I could exchange some of the paintings whenever I wanted to. He also encouraged me to come down and spend a week or two as an artist-in-residence, telling me that the loft in the gallery had a complete artist workshop with sleeping accommodations. I told him I would have to think about it. After Chuck and I left, I remember thinking how strangely this entire situation had come about. I actually wondered if this was in fact being orchestrated by divine intervention because the events were so unusual.

Bill seemed like an honest person, and I felt comfortable in his presence. His eyes looked sad, and I sensed he was a lonely man, even though he tried to cover it up by joking all the time. He was rather nice-looking, with dark brown hair neatly combed to the side. I could tell he loved the outdoors because he had a dark tan. Another distinct feature was his meticulous attire. He gave the appearance of a distinguished person in an *Esquire* magazine.

Once I returned home, Bill began calling me often. At first, it was to discuss business. Then he wanted to know when I was coming back to Galveston. I told him I did not want to drive that far by myself and that I was afraid to drive through Houston. He persisted, and after two weeks of prodding, I agreed to come down and spend a week as an artist-in-residence to make the long drive down there worthwhile.

Since it was my first time to drive through the city of Houston, I considered it a nightmare of highways and unbelievable traffic. My legs were shaking, and my hands were white-knuckled as I clutched the steering wheel in a vise-like grip. By the time I arrived at the gallery five and a half hours later, I was exhausted, but I willed myself to calm down.

As soon as I entered the gallery, a steady flow of other merchants began coming in to meet the artist-in-residence. I knew they were curious and wanted to meet the artist Bill had talked about. People kept dropping in until Bill closed the gallery at five o'clock that night.

While there, I set up and painted every day. Bill even sold one of my paintings. After one of his busiest days, Bill took me for a walk on the beach and we watched the sunset. Afterwards, he took me out to dinner before taking me back to the gallery. In the mornings, we met for breakfast and returned to the gallery. Another morning, Bill insisted we take a boat ride to look at the sunrise before going to his favorite restaurant for breakfast. It was the first time I had done that, and we both decided to do it again before I left. By the time the week ended, I was not anxious to leave, but I had to get back to Austin to get ready for a solo art show. Before leaving, I promised Bill I would come back soon. As it turned out, I traveled to Galveston every weekend for five weeks.

My big art show was scheduled to open in another month, and Bill promised he would come for the opening. In July 1984, Bill flew to Austin, arriving the day before the show. I went over all the preparations to make sure I had not forgotten anything. Getting ready for a solo art show involves much planning and last minute decisions. The idea that Bill would be there made me a bit nervous, and that night I was unable to sleep.

I should not have worried so much because the show turned out to be the best I ever had. The seventy-five guests enjoyed a variety of appetizers and wine as they walked around looking at the paintings. Opening night, I sold six paintings, and by the time the show came down a month later, I had sold fifteen of the twenty-three paintings on display. To top it off, I was asked to do three paintings on commission.

The day after the show, Bill had to leave because he was the only one who worked in his gallery. Our time together had been fun but not what I would consider a romantic get-together. When we parted at the airport, I did not feel the usual love palpitations in my heart or a sense of loss that usually goes along with a new romance. I was grateful that we had become close friends, knowing we had much in common. In fact, I learned that Bill was also interested in photography and had won a first place award in the local art competition a few years before I met him.

As I watched him leave, I had to admit that I was on my guard. I did not want a serious relationship. Frankly, I had made up my mind that driving to Galveston every week was too much trouble, and I was going to have to cut down on those excursions. I enjoyed being single and the freedom I was now accustomed to. The last thing I wanted was a serious relationship. I had made up my mind that I did not want to get married again.

Several months later, his mother went to visit him and planned to stay a week. Towards the middle of the week, Bill called and asked me to come down because he wanted me to meet his mother. He told me he had not been feeling well the entire time she had been there and was sad because he had not been able to take her to her favorite places. He pleaded with me, saying he wanted his mother to meet me and wanted us to have some fun together. After thinking it over, I finally relented and left on Friday to spend the weekend.

The next day, after lunch, Bill asked me to take his mother for a ride on the beach so she could spend time looking for seashells—her favorite thing to do. He told us he would take a nap while we were gone. His mother was worried, saying Bill did not feel well, and she did not feel comfortable leaving him alone. When Bill heard this, he went to his room and closed the door.

In a short time, we heard a terrible sound coming from the bedroom. His mother and I jumped up and ran to his room to find Bill thrashing on the bed, delirious and vomiting. He did not respond when we called his name. Luckily, he had shown me a paper next to his phone in the kitchen that listed phone numbers and his address, in case I ever needed it. I dialed 911 and was able to give them the address. I told them I would wait for them on the sidewalk in front of his apartment because, being a huge apartment complex, all the units looked alike.

In less than five minutes, the ambulance arrived. The EMS people ran upstairs with a gurney and immediately checked Bill's vital signs, gave him a shot of something, then rushed him downstairs on the gurney. They placed him in the ambulance and began working on him again before leaving. This gave his mother and me the chance to get into my car so I could follow the ambulance. I stayed close behind them, hoping I would remember the way back to the apartment. My heart raced as I sped to keep up with the ambulance.

We were two scared women, babbling incoherently, out of our minds with worry, wondering what would happen next. I parked the car while they rushed Bill into the emergency room. Once inside, we were told to sit in the waiting room, that someone would come to talk to us after Bill was stabilized. We waited three hours without being approached by anyone. His mother was beside herself with worry and went to look for a nurse to ask what the heck was going on. When she came back with a nurse, I was told to follow them into the emergency room.

The doctor on duty told us that Bill had suffered a cardiac arrest. His heart had stopped twice while he was in the ambulance and had stopped again in the emergency room. They had to apply electric paddles each time to start his heart. His mother was told that Bill had heart damage and would be in the hospital for at least a week in order to have some tests run. They moved Bill to a private room and told us to leave because he needed to rest.

I retraced the route we had taken to the hospital and found the apartment without any trouble. On the way back, like a pressure valve that has been released, Mrs. Howland began sobbing and cried all the way home. She kept repeating what a blessing it was that I had come down for the weekend—that it had to have been divine intervention because, had she been alone, she would not have known what to do. I was surprised when I heard her say that.

She began repeating in-between sobs, "Don't leave! Oh, God. Please don't leave me alone! I don't know what to do! I don't know my way around Galveston, and if you leave, I'll be lost. I need you, and so does Bill. I know he would want you to be here by his side when he feels better, so please say you'll stay."

I tried to calm her by agreeing to stay as long as I was needed. As the doctor predicted, Bill was in the hospital one week. While he was there, we spent every day with him. We were in his room most of the day and only left briefly for lunch and dinner. Then we'd return and spend several more hours at night. After he was released from the hospital, we actually had some free time whenever Bill took a nap. As he began feeling better, I decided to return to Austin. I had not planned on being gone for such a long time. By the end of the second week, I could see that they could manage without me and I drove back home.

The doctor told Bill he would not be able to return to work for at least three months. While I was away, Mrs. Howland went to the gallery every day to oversee the situation and to check the books. She told Bill that the gallery would have to close because he could not continue to pay the exorbitant rent each month. Mrs. Howland had to return to Florida and could not take on the burden at her age. Bill called me and asked if I could possibly return to Galveston to help him. Somehow, I could not refuse, and I drove down to spend a few days. Thanksgiving was the following week, and I invited Bill and his mother to Austin as my houseguests. The Monday after Thanksgiving, I drove them back to Galveston and spent four days trying to help them resolve the many problems they now faced. When I returned to Austin, I purposely did not go back to Galveston.

By now, Bill felt well enough to take his mother to the airport, and she went back to Florida. He was also well enough to handle his many responsibilities in disposing of the gallery. He called all the artists who were displaying there and informed them that he was closing the gallery for health reasons. He emphasized that their artwork had to be taken out within the next two weeks.

As soon as he had taken care of business in Galveston, Bill returned to Austin. I had agreed for him to move in with me temporarily. I made it clear that, whenever his doctor gave him permission to go back to work, he would have to start looking for a job. I wrote a rental agreement, stating he could begin paying me a reasonable rent whenever he started working again. I knew that, being in poor health, he would need time to recuperate. He had nowhere to go and no job in sight. The dye was cast.

Two months later, Bill received permission from his doctor to return to work. He applied for jobs every day, but everywhere he went, they told him the same thing; he was overqualified. He did not want to give up looking, but after many interviews and rejections, he became discouraged and quit looking. He told me he could not think of what to do next. Before long, I saw signs that he was very depressed.

During our months together, we had had many conversations about Bill's past. He had told me he had served in the United States Navy during the Korean War. After the war, he went to college and received a BS degree in animal husbandry. He then became the manager of a huge dairy farm in Maryland. When that contract expired, a firm that sold mice and rats for cancer research hired him.

He later took courses at the Goodwin Institute at Nova University in Florida and at Notre Dame University, which specialized in cancer research for developing germ-free mice. This later led him to a position as manager of a lab in the Houston area where they raised germ-free mice, then sold them to cancer research labs. After several years in that position, he decided to retire. He waited a year before deciding to use his life's savings to open the gallery in Galveston.

In thinking back about what he had told me, I realized that of course he was overqualified for a job selling cars or apparel in a department store. With his background, he was looking in the wrong places. I wondered what I could do to help his situation. In my daily hour of meditation, which had become a habit, I focused on asking for guidance that would help us find a solution to his problem. Before too long, an idea began forming in my mind. During my long career as an artist, I had often thought about the possibility of starting a business that would make use of my paintings. An idea that seemed workable was taking form, but I wanted to think about it more clearly before mentioning it to Bill.

I was aware that it would present a huge challenge and would be a financial risk for me. But my intuition was telling me to go ahead and take a chance because you never know what you can accomplish until you try. I spent the next three weeks thinking about what I should do. Like a revelation, it finally dawned on me! I was thinking only about the reasons why my ideas wouldn't work instead of thinking of ways to make them work. With this new attitude and confidence, I approached Bill with my plan. I knew it was one that could be developed within a month or two if I allowed myself to be led by divine guidance.

New ideas were coming to me like the flow of a waterfall. As I thought of new solutions, I talked them over with Bill and got his input. We spent hours discussing ways to implement our combined ideas. The air became charged with a surge of power that I cannot even define. We were so filled with excitement. Our waking hours became packed with activities that filled us with a renewed youthfulness. We were like kids again, laughing and looking forward to each new day. Our time together cemented our friendship, and we became inseparable.

Back in the 1970s, I had purchased one acre of waterfront property on Canyon Lake, and the property value had increased considerably. I went to my bank and asked if I could use it as collateral for a business loan. I spoke with the president, and together, we negotiated a loan that I qualified for. Next, I went to the City Hall in Austin and I applied for a tax permit and filed a DBA. We named our company Lucille Enterprises. It would feature Texas gifts. Our goal was to promote our products as a means of educating the public about Texas facts. By following my intuition, my ideas were being implemented almost effortlessly.

When you're in the flow, things have a way of happening that amazes you. We wasted no time in locating a well-respected printing company in Austin that published magazines. After meeting with the president, he agreed to make prints of two of my Texas-themed paintings, even though that was not what they normally did. The reason we contacted them was because we wanted to advertise our prints in their Austin and San Antonio magazines.

Since making color separations is a complicated and precise procedure, it required many meetings with the staff and the president. After several months, the negatives were approved, the ads followed, and the prints went into production. On completion, both prints were an exact replica of my paintings. The first watercolor painting was of the State Capitol in Austin superimposed in front of the Texas flag. The second painting depicted an enlarged version of the State of Texas with vignettes depicting important scenes from various areas around the state. Both prints became popular sale items in our Lucille Enterprises venture.

Sales were so good that we decided to have the pictures reproduced on a smaller scale and sell them as refrigerator magnets. Bill got busy setting up a workshop in our garage, cutting 2 ½" x 3 ½" pieces of Masonite boards by the hundreds. He later glued the pictures on them and covered the pictures with a high-gloss finish. Within a month, we were in full production, selling Texas-theme magnets by the dozens.

Bill became our company salesman and covered all the gift shops in Austin and San Antonio. As our sales increased, I spent every day thinking up new ideas to expand our company products. We decided to have our designs silk-screened onto T-shirts. We spent months doing research. Getting our designs silk-screened proved to be a mammoth undertaking because the designs involved making a screen for each color and ours required five. We bought T-shirts by the gross, had them printed, and ended up with too many rejects because the silk-screening was of poor quality. We wasted a lot of money before we finally located a reliable silk-screener who was capable of reproducing our fine designs.

I continued to paint, creating new designs for the company. During our second year in business, we hired a woman to help us. She turned out to be a fast learner and was capable in every aspect of our productions. She reduced our workload considerably.

Traveling with Bill on one of his sales trips around Texas, the mesmerizing spring scenery called to me. An idea for a new painting began to form in my mind. I couldn't wait to get home and start a watercolor. I painted the top half of the Texas flag, featuring the enlarged blue section with a large star in the middle. Inside the star, I painted a landscape with bluebonnets—the Texas flower. Below the blue section, I painted the red and white sections of the flag.

We decided to produce prints of this new painting onto notepaper, along with prints of the Capitol and the Texas state design. These three designs helped us expand our business greatly. Soon we hired a seamstress, who made tote bags and duffle bags to add to our inventory. We ordered labels made with our company name that included: "Made in Texas by Texans." The seamstress sewed them on all the fabric items.

Bill surprised me on my birthday that year with a 14-karat blue topaz pendant (the Texas gem stone) set in a lovely gold setting. The topaz pendant was so gorgeous; I decided to do a painting of it.

At first, I did a rough sketch. Then I arrived at a design I knew would be breathtaking. I drew the topaz in the middle of a full sheet of watercolor paper 22" x 30" and tried to capture its many facets. The next day, I began painting the topaz with the various hues I could see, and with a freedom of expression, I painted bluebonnets below the topaz. They formed the shape of fingers that seemed to hold the stone. Wow! The simplicity and beauty was dazzling, indeed, breathtaking. It now became one of our more popular designs. We had it silk-screened on all the cloth items, which now also included sweatshirts.

We started participating in the craft shows that were held in the Palmer Auditorium in Austin. The exposure was an excellent means of showing and selling our products. At one of the shows, we learned about the Dallas World Trade Center. Many of the gift shop owners encouraged us to visit the complex, telling us it would be a great way for us to become better known. As members, our company would have professional status. We began making inquiries and registered our company with the Dallas World Trade Center that year.

A few months later, we attended our first big world market event. We located a hotel nearby and looked forward to the trip because it would give us time for much-needed rest and relaxation. Our first day in the Dallas Market was taken up mainly with finding our way around the place. It was such a huge complex.

On our second day, being familiar with the layout, we concentrated on calling on showrooms that handled only gift items. The last showroom we visited was the largest and had twelve salespeople. Luckily, we recently had a three-page color brochure printed that showed all the products we carried. This had made it easier for Bill to show our products when he called on gift shops. When the salespeople began looking at the brochure and the wide variety of Texas gifts, they were greatly impressed. The brochure created such excitement that other salespeople began gathering around, wanting to look for themselves. The charged atmosphere and loud conversation brought the manager out of his office, curious to see what the commotion was all about.

After looking at our brochure of Texas gifts, he too, was impressed, especially since they did not carry Texas gift items. He immediately saw that adding our line would greatly improve sales for their showroom and told us he wanted to carry our products on an exclusive basis. This meant Bill would no longer have to call on our existing accounts, and it would give him more time to devote to purchasing, producing, and shipping orders. Talk about an answer that would ease our workload.

During a late lunch break, we discussed the details with the manager, and after being served lunch, we signed a contract to be exclusively represented by their showroom. We later met with our sales representative and made plans with him for our next meeting. Since he worked strictly on a commission basis, he would also get the future commissions Bill had worked so hard to establish. We understood that the volume of added accounts and sales would more than make up for the commissions we paid out. Bill was now free to be home full time, and he could devote more time to the countless projects our business was generating.

Our products were suddenly very popular because there were not very many businesses that made or distributed Texas gifts. Even though we had many designs and products, we were required to come up with new products every year. With this in mind, we were constantly thinking of ways to add new items to our business.

We had been thinking about adding ceramic items with bluebonnets on them, and after months of searching, we located a couple that owned a mom-and-pop ceramic shop in Austin. We arranged to meet with them, and they agreed to make our exclusive items that featured only bluebonnets. Every month, we added one or two new pieces, until we had close to fifty. This new line of Texas gifts increased our workload tremendously. We had to go to the ceramic shop to wrap each order separately, carry the orders home, and then repack each order in shipping boxes to be picked up by UPS at our house later on.

On one of our visits to the Dallas World Trade Center, I noticed that potpourri had become a popular item. When we returned to Austin, I began investigating where to buy some bluebonnet potpourri. I was told there was none. I located a place where potpourri was manufactured and ordered a mix. Bill and I helped create an unusual scent and had it added to the mix of our selected chips and flowers. As far as I know, that became the first bluebonnet potpourri. My next project was to find a company that made labels and a company that carried small plastic bags the size we needed. We eventually found a label company in California and a plastic bag manufacturer in Texas. Our potpourri mix with the added scent was shipped to us in huge barrels.

Working in our garage, Bill, Alicia, and I formed an assembly line. One person packed the potpourri in the small plastic bag; the next twisted the top and sealed it with scotch tape, then tied a gold cord with a bow that gave it a nice finished look. The gold label I designed had embossed bluebonnets in royal blue, and our company name was added in a lovely script. The lower portion said, "Made in Texas by Texans." My job was to place the label on the front of the bag because this required a steady hand. When the stores displayed them by the cash register, the scent was impossible to resist and they sold out right away. All the gift shops reordered them by the gross, they sold out so fast.

One of the other salesmen in the Dallas showroom lived in Louisiana, and seeing how well our products sold, asked if we could create special designs for Louisiana. We went into production and came up with several designs. The most popular was a Mardi grass design. We later introduced a potpourri for Louisiana, but it did not sell well. That was our first disappointment.

* * *

On my birthday in June, Bill presented me with a small box. When I opened it, I was surprised to find an engagement ring. It was a gorgeous emerald surrounded by diamonds. Knowing that Mother and George and my brother Emile and Aunt Lucy were all coming for Christmas and to arrive on December 19, Bill and I decided to have our wedding December 21. My daughters Debbie and Linda were excited about the big event and sent out invitations to our closest friends.

They insisted on having a lavish reception after the wedding ceremony in Cass and Debbie's lovely home. They ordered a beautiful three-tiered wedding cake with a bride and groom perched on top, and instead of wedding gifts, the guests gave us a money tree. The only disappointment was that my son Arty and his wife Peggy could not attend. As we sped off to our honeymoon suite, Bill and I talked about the fact that we had been together for four years. Our business had kept us so busy that the years had flown by.

Our business continued to prosper for the next four years. By the middle of 1992, the economy began to slump and many businesses began cutting down on purchasing gift items. As our business declined, we had to drop out of the showroom in Dallas. Bill went back to dealing directly with our many loyal customers. When business declined even more, we had to lay off Alicia, our only employee. Within a month, it was obvious that it was too much for Bill and me to keep up with the workload. We tried to hang in there for a while longer, but being in our mid-sixties, the idea of retiring looked more appealing.

Our business venture had been a tremendous success, giving us a steady income and many unforgettable years of excitement. But, as my intuition began prodding me that the time had arrived to end it, I knew that my spiritual guardian was providing me with guidance I was to follow. After discussing it with Bill, we agreed that the prospects of staying in business were looking mighty grim, and we spent the next six months contacting all our accounts to notify them that we were closing. We sold off the existing inventory as best we could and terminated our ceramic business. Closing down a business, we learned, was very involved, and by the middle of 1995, we had completed the last requirements. The day we finalized everything, Bill and I went out to dinner and celebrated.

22

A GIFT FROM BEYOND

In 1992 George passed away unexpectedly. He had brought so much joy to our family that we missed him terribly. Mother found it difficult to live by herself and far from any relatives, therefore, a year later she moved to Tampa to be close to her grandson Richard. They had always been extremely close, so becoming her caregiver was a role he enthusiastically accepted. She had practically raised him as a boy, and while he was in high school, he had lived with her. Actually, Richard was more like a son than a grandson.

Mother also wanted to keep the tradition of visiting us for the month of July, as she had done each year with George. As July approached in 1994, she asked her sister, my Aunt Lucy, to come with her to Texas. I agreed that this would make it extra special. I looked forward to their visit, recalling how contagious Mother's laugh was; that invariably made her the life of any party. I knew that having them spend a month would only bring back the happy times we missed.

The first week they were with us, we relaxed and spent most of the time visiting with the rest of the family. While we were having breakfast one morning, Mother surprised me by saying she was thinking seriously of moving to Texas, adding that she wanted to live with me. That was something I had often longed for, and I was thrilled. But I knew that, in order for that to happen, I would have to sell my two-story house because Mother was already having difficulty climbing stairs.

Within a few days, we began taking daily trips traveling around Austin and the outlying areas, looking at single-story houses for sale. Nothing we looked at was suitable. We spent nearly the entire time of their visit doing this. The week before they were to leave, we went to a Jim's Restaurant for lunch. In the entrance, I picked up a real estate brochure and, while waiting for our food, began looking through it. There were two houses listed for sale that looked promising in an area I was not familiar with. It was in the Hill Country northwest of Austin overlooking Lake Travis. As soon as we returned home, I called the listing agent and arranged for us to meet her the next day.

As it turned out, the two houses the brochure featured did not fit our requirements at all. We were disappointed, but it had given us the opportunity to see the beautiful area. Hearing our comments, the agent decided to drive us around to show us other lots for sale. She told us the builder that she worked with could build us a house on any lot we chose.

As we crested a hill, the magnificent view in the distance took my breath away. My intuition went into overdrive, and my body tingled with excitement. I knew immediately we had found the place I had been looking for. Again, I'm certain that my spiritual guardian had led me to an area I did not even know existed. Bill, Mother, and Lucy were overwhelmed by the view the lot provided. We walked around the lot and decided this was where we wanted to live. We went to the office and spoke with the builder, who showed us plans for several houses, and I selected one that could be modified to my specifications. The following weekend, Mother and Lucy had to leave for the long drive back to Florida.

After they left, I called a real estate agent, and the next day I signed a contract to sell my house. Within six months, the house sold with a contingency clause pending the completion of the house we were building. The entire time the new house was being built, Mother stayed busy packing all her belongings in boxes and stacking them in her living room.

Bill took pictures of the different stages of construction, and I mailed them to Mother to give her the chance to see the monthly progress and the finished results. It took a year for the house to be completed. As the closing day approached, Mother began giving away some of her things and sold most of her furniture. She kept her bedroom set and a few other items she wanted for her room. The week before she was to move, she went to a U-Haul company with her grandson and paid for the rental of a truck. She was really anxious to move and looked forward to living in Texas.

We moved into our new house the day before Easter in 1995. The entire family pitched in to help us get the house in order. Linda and Debbie took care of the kitchen, and by nightfall, the entire house was furnished as if we had lived in it for a year. Unbelievably, we had our traditional Easter gathering with the twenty-two family members in our new house.

The following two days, Bill and I stayed busy with the finishing touches and emptied the room that would become Mother's room. By Tuesday night, we were finished and went to bed around midnight totally exhausted. Within an hour, someone rang the doorbell. We had just moved in, so my first thought was that it must be a robber checking to see if the house was unoccupied. We waited, and a second later, the doorbell rang again. This time, Bill and I jumped out of bed, and Bill cautiously went to see who was at the door. He was shocked to find our daughter Debbie.

When we moved into our house, the builder had neglected to notice that being in a rural area we had no a telephone pole near the house. The phone company promised to install one in a few weeks. Our not having a telephone forced Debbie to drive that long distance in the middle of the night. When she walked into the house, she immediately told me to sit down. Without prolonging the inevitable, she informed us that my mother had died unexpectedly in her chair that morning and had not been discovered until later that night. I began screaming and sobbing uncontrollably and could not stop.

Debbie stayed as long as she could to console me, but I was in such a state of shock and disbelief that no one could penetrate my anguish. Debbie had to leave soon afterwards to be with her own family and to deal with her own grief after losing her precious grandmother in such an unexpected way. In her state of mind, I have no idea how she was able to drive that long distance in the pitch darkness.

She left me her cell phone so I could call my nephew Richard in Florida. He told me that when he went to check on Mother, he looked through the window blinds and saw her slumped in her chair, as if she were sleeping.

He let himself in and called EMS and then my brother Emile, who lived in St. Petersburg.

The next day Bill and I left for Florida and arrived on Friday. We met with the funeral home director and later greeted the relatives who had already begun to gather. Debbie and Linda flew to Florida together and joined us later on Friday. Being with them gave me the strength and comfort I desperately needed. To compound the sadness, the funeral took place on Sunday, which was Mother's Day.

After we returned home, I could not come to grips with my grief. I cried nonstop for days. I thought about countless memories and reflected on the fun times I had shared with my mother and George. A particular visit we had one July flashed through my mind.

It had been George's seventy-fifth birthday, and Mother and I had gone shopping for a special birthday gift. Not knowing what to buy him, I suggested we stop at my favorite place, the Artisans' Alley in San Antonio. The shops are a co-op of artists who are known for making unusual gifts. In one of the rooms, I spotted something I felt was the perfect gift for George. I shouted across the room, "Mother, come here and look at this! I'm going to buy it."

It was a triangle-shaped hand-tooled pendant made of hammered silver, and superimposed on the front was the large Roman numeral number *one* made of brass. It really stood out against the silver. Mother was thrilled at my find, and she bought a silver chain for it. When we gave it to George, he put it around his neck as soon as he saw it, and from that moment on, he wore it all the time. He never took it off, not even when he showered. He loved his gift, and kiddingly, he would pound his chest and with a big grin and a twinkle in his eye, he would say, "I'm number one!"

He made us laugh, and we told him he was indeed our number one person in the family. That pendant became George's most prized possession.

After George died, Mother cleaned the pendant and wore it around her neck. Like George, she never took it off. It became her most treasured piece of jewelry. The memory of it brought on a flood of tears, and for several months, I could not stop crying.

One night I was feeling especially sad and decided to go out on the back deck of the house. I was standing by the railing with a glass of wine when my gaze shifted to the dark sky above me. The million stars overhead sparkled like diamonds. The sight of them reminded me of my mother because many years before someone had nicknamed her "Diamond Lil" and we often called her by that endearing name. As I stood sipping my wine, I could not believe she was gone. As I thought of her, questions began forming in my mind.

Where was she? Could she hear me?

Then a conversation we had had about life after death many years earlier popped into my head. She, like Art, had told me, if it was possible to contact each other after we die, that she would find a way to do so. Looking up at the stars, I shouted as loudly as I could, "Mother, if you can hear me, please send me a sign!"

Nothing happened, but a sense of calm came over me, and for the first time in months, I stopped crying. I went back inside and told Bill what I had done. Instinctively, I knew it was important for him to know what I had said.

The next morning, while walking to the corner mailbox, my eyes were drawn to an orange stone among thousands of white ones on the ground. I had a sudden urge to pick it up but ignored it and kept walking. Several more times, as I walked back from the mailboxes, I felt a strong urge to find the stone but chose to ignore it. When I finally returned to my doorstep, a strong sensation like someone pushing me and telling me to go back and pick up that stone made me retrace my steps.

The orange stone was easy to spot among the white ones, so I picked it up. It wasn't until I turned it over that I saw in the middle of the stone was the Roman numeral *one* permanently etched into the stone.

It was exactly like the one on Mother's pendant. Only Mother would have known that the number one would be a sign that I would immediately recognize. Mother's smiling face flashed before me, and in my mind, I heard her say, "Here is your sign, my dear."

The stone I held in my hand was a tangible object and proof to me that our souls *do* live on after we die. My search for the meaning of life was answered: We are infinite!

That night, as I lay in bed staring at a bright light, a foggy mist appeared, and I went into that familiar trance state. In a short time, I sensed my spiritual guardian transferring his thoughts to me.

The words were a reminder of the vision I had had many years before, when he had told me I had a mission to accomplish. His message could not have been clearer.

"Your mission is to tell your story. It must be told in order to inspire others to seek the gift of divine guidance that is available to everyone."

* * *

ABOUT THE AUTHOR

Lucille Edgarian is a professional artist, author, and entrepreneur. Born in the industrial metropolis of Manchester, New Hampshire, at the height of the Great Depression, she developed from a shy ward of the state to a successful businesswoman, in spite of her humble beginnings. Her parents separated before Lucille was two years old, forcing her mother to seek assistance from a Catholic convent. This and other events, such as the onset of World War II, created opportunities for Lucille to live in many places and to meet interesting people. In addition, several marriages and family added depth to her character and a spiritual strength that has guided her throughout her life.

Recognized at points in her career in both the *Notable Women of Texas* and *Who's Who of Women Executives*, Lucille's formal art education includes training at the American Society of Fine Arts and at the Corcoran Gallery of Art in Washington, D.C. While living in Pordenone, Italy, she also became the first female apprentice to one of Italy's most noted artists, Professor Pio Rossi. She has received numerous awards from juried art competitions and is a signature member of the Texas Watercolor Society. Lucille also taught watercolor, acrylic, and oil painting classes for over thirty years. In 2007 she was invited to participate in the New York Art Expo held in the Javits Convention Center. Her work was featured in the Art-Exchange showroom. She is a past president of the San Antonio Chapter of the National Society of Arts and Letters and was the national art chairman for the organization. Her artwork is now represented in many corporate and private collections internationally.

At one point in her career, Lucille was a licensed real estate agent in Texas, but in 1986 she decided to leave real estate and form her own company. She and her husband, Bill Howland, created Lucille Enterprises, a company that manufactured Texas gift items featuring some of Lucille's artwork. Currently, Lucille resides in the Texas Hill Country with its magnificent vista views and beautiful lake. She continues to paint and write, and enjoys keeping up with her three children, six grandchildren, and six great-grandchildren.